Big Ideas for Small Businesses

BIG IDEAS
for Small Businesses
A Desktop Guide for Entrepreneurs

Norton Paley

Viva Books

New Delhi | Mumbai | Chennai | Kolkata | Bengaluru | Hyderabad | Kochi | Guwahati

Publisher's note

First Published 2011
Reprinted 2014

Viva Books Private Limited

4737/23, Ansari Road, Daryaganj, New Delhi 110 002
Tel. 42242200, 23258325, 23283121, Email: vivadelhi@vivagroupindia.net

76, Service Industries, Shirvane, Sector 1, Nerul, Navi Mumbai 400 706
Tel. 27721273, 27721274, Email: vivamumbai@vivagroupindia.net

Jamals Fazal Chambers, 26 Greams Road, Chennai 600 006
Tel. 28294241, 28290304, Email: vivachennai@vivagroupindia.net

B-103, Jindal Towers, 21/1A/3 Darga Road, Kolkata 700 017
Tel. 22816713, Email: vivakolkata@vivagroupindia.net

7, GF, Sovereign Park Aptts., 56-58, K. R. Road, Basavanagudi, Bengaluru 560 004
Tel. 26607409, Email: vivabangalore@vivagroupindia.net

101-102, Moghal Marc Apartments, 3-4-637 to 641, Narayanguda, Hyderabad 500 029
Tel. 27564481, Email: vivahyderabad@vivagroupindia.net

First Floor, Beevi Towers, SRM Road, Kaloor, Kochi 682 018
Tel. 0484-2403055, 2403056, Email: vivakochi@vivagroupindia.net

232, GNB Road, Beside UCO Bank, Silpukhuri, Guwahati 781 003
Tel. 0361-2666386, Email: vivaguwahati@vivagroupindia.net

www.vivagroupindia.com

ISBN: 978-81-309-1714-6

Published by Vinod Vasishtha for Viva Books Private Limited
4737/23 Ansari Road, Daryaganj, New Delhi 110 002.

Printed & bound by Raj Press, R-3, Inderpuri, New Delhi 110 012.

M0000/M0220

Dedication

To Annette, with love.

Contents

Introduction

Why is it that some companies overcome huge obstacles and achieve spectacular successes and others are giant failures?

Is it mere luck that some entrepreneurs continue to outperform their competitors, while others toil in leftover, barely profitable segments?

Don't the winning and losing business owners and managers face similar obstacles?

They confront competition on a daily basis, feel the impact of rising costs and reduced profits, and struggle to find innovative products and services before rivals beat them to market.

They also must compete in an ongoing battle for funds to run their businesses and react to the unrelenting demands for increased sales and profits.

The risks are high and real. Money is spent. People are committed in a challenge that means the triumph or downfall of a company, along with their hopes and dreams. Yet, given all or few of those barriers, some companies continue to thrive while others washout or just plod along year after year.

In the end, however, it is a manager's ability to respond correctly to the changing dynamics of a competitive marketplace, the know-how to develop a quality business plan, and the skill to successfully develop business-building strategies that determine success.

Big Ideas for Small Businesses is positioned to (1) provide you with the skills and tools to grow your business; and (2) show you how to inspire your people to actively pursue opportunities for growth.

To that end, this book is developed on the following six realities:

1. Rigorous business principles do exist and need to be followed regardless of your type of business.
2. Well thought-out business plans backed by reliable market and competitor intelligence are essential prerequisites before committing any amount of resources.
3. Implementing even the most basic competitive strategies requires well-honed leadership talent and a superior ability to motivate employees.
4. Effective decision-making depends on nurturing a customer-driven company culture consisting of core values that are unique to your firm. These values become the essential underpinnings if you are to expect winning performance from your employees.
5. Full-grown efficiencies rely on persistently searching inside and outside your industry for best practices, then benchmarking them selectively for application to your firm.
6. Looking for fresh opportunities requires you to use a wide-vision lens. As geographic distances dissolve and cultural distances emerge, they materialize as the more important possibilities for growth.

CHAPTER OUTLINE

Chapter 1. Outthink, Outmaneuver, Outperform Competition

The chapter opens with case examples of extraordinary individuals from diverse, and in some cases humble backgrounds, who went on to develop start-up companies that accomplished some of the most outstanding business successes of the last 75 years. All of them shared characteristics of ambition, courage, and tenacity.

Their remarkable achievements serve as the entry point for a list of 22 management ideas. If incorporated into your business, they can position your company to reach new levels of growth and opportunity.

Chapter 2. Develop a Positive Mindset and Attitude

Here, you delve into the human elements of managing. Find out how an individual's attitude, state of mind, and overall way of thinking can decide the outcome of your plans.

Learn how to take a broad look at behavior and the possibilities of changing your staff's mindset and outlook. That means inspiring those who are generally positive and compliant, the not-so-compliant, individuals with negative feelings, and even persons with insubordinate behavior.

Chapter 3. Project Optimistic Leadership

Leadership and managerial performance contain learned skills. These include such positive attributes as insightfulness, compassion, boldness, and strictness. You are shown how to apply them to the realities of creating opportunities in a tough competitive environment. And if the acquired skills merge with your innate talents, then you are likely to become an outstanding leader, clearly distinguishable from a mediocre manager.

Chapter 4. Create Competitive Strategies and Tactics

In aggressively contested marketplaces where competing managers are often pitted against each other, you learn the actions and counteractions that can outthink, outmaneuver, and outwin your rivals and achieve success.

It is by mastering the rules of strategies and tactics that you will survive the tough times, gain ground over competitors, and maintain a pathway to growth.

Chapter 5. Decode Your Competitors

Decoding competitors encompasses one central idea: If you know your rival's plans, you are better able to monitor his moves. Then you can estimate, with some degree of accuracy, which strategies are likely to succeed and reject those with minimal chances of success.

Therefore, you want to be fully acquainted with the overall strategies and short-term actions of your competitor. With the tools and guidelines provided for gathering competitor intelligence, you can immediately begin the systematic process of decoding competitors.

Chapter 6. Distinguish Your Business

With today's markets in a state of flux, numerous companies are restructuring their organizations, revamping their strategies, and realigning their staffs. It is in those vacant gaps that you can discover opportunities in once overlooked niches that now may be open to you.

To exploit the openings, you are given a variety of options, guidelines, and problem-solving techniques to distinguish your business and commit to action.

Chapter 7. Segment Your Markets

Subdividing the market helps immeasurably in strengthening your market position, even against a larger competitor. Here, you are shown traditional, as well as advanced techniques for splitting your market into smaller segments. Doing so permits you to concentrate resources for maximum effect. Meaning: You improve your chances to identify clusters of individuals in emerging, neglected, or overlooked segments.

You are also given a 100-question strength/weakness checklist. This set of guidelines lets you conduct a total assessment of your company's ability to reach intended markets, maintain effective customer relationships, and challenge competitors. The process also furnishes you with a constructive look at your company's overall competencies.

Chapter 8. Create an Effective Business Plan

The Strategic Business Plan is the essential document to give your organization direction and purpose. Further, it provides the agility to "flip from a long-term strategy to the nuts and bolts of everyday planning."

You are given a flexible format for developing your plan, which is a starting place for identifying opportunities and developing strategies. The plan thereby becomes your route map.

SPECIAL FEATURE

Strategy Diagnostic Tool

As business plans succeed or fail according to the best-practiced rules of strategy, you can draw on a unique diagnostic tool to assess the risks and overall viability of your competitive strategies. Use it to provide a reliable performance measure to gauge the likelihood of success, before you commit resources.

HOW TO GET THE MOST FROM THIS BOOK

You can use this book in several ways:

1. Read it cover-to-cover in the sequence the book was written and acquire the foundation concepts and techniques to grow your business.
2. Jump into the book at any point and go directly to the topic that is most pressing and gain mental nourishment and skill improvement for your own situation.
3. Randomly go through the chapters and tap into the numerous checklists and bulleted guidelines that summarize the key ideas of the section.

4. Look at the case examples used throughout the book for ideas and examples of best practices. In some instances, large companies are cited, if they illustrate the points being made.

These case examples are valid if you consider that many big businesses consist of a bundle of smaller operations identified as divisions, business units, departments, or product lines.

Each operation typically functions with its own budget, markets its own distinct products to a defined customer segment, and faces a unique set of competitors. For funding, each manager presents a business plan to senior management, which serves as a "banker".

Good luck!

1

Outthink, Outmaneuver, Outperform Competition

How did some of the business greats of the past 75 years achieve extraordinary success? What can you learn from their careers to help you outthink, outmaneuver, and outperform your competitors? What can you discover about creating opportunities in a tough environment?

The following case examples describe individuals from widely diverse backgrounds, some from impoverished surroundings, who realized amazing triumphs. They all shared commonalities:

First, all began their careers as start-up businesses. Second, ambition, courage, and tenacity were their most visible personal traits.

Following their stories, you will find a list of 22 management ideas. Once you review the ideas, selectively merge them with the key lessons from the cases. You are then likely to find enough grist to energize your thinking and move your firm forward to fresh opportunities.

David Sarnoff of RCA commanded what was called, "an Invisible Empire of the Air, intangible, yet solid as granite." The company, under Sarnoff's guidance and stewardship, became the foundation for today's electronic mass media.

His unique qualities included the ability to act as a visionary, builder, and leader. At the early age of 15 and at the turn of the twentieth century, Sarnoff stumbled onto a revolutionary technology – the wireless telegraph. With zealous enthusiasm he immersed himself in all that was known about the new mode of communications.

In particular, it was the applications that fascinated Sarnoff; especially the potential of marrying wireless communication to the emerging industry of radio. More precisely, he focused on the refined application of radio where he envisioned growth – public entertainment.

Sarnoff expressed his vision this way, "I have in mind a plan of development which would make radio a household utility in the same sense as the piano or the phonograph. The idea is to bring music into the home by wireless."

Sarnoff's foresight became a reality when General Electric formed RCA. It was at that key point in 1920 that he shaped his vision in a detailed business plan. By 1926, five million American homes had radios and commercial programming grew by leaps and bounds, proliferating through every facet of public and consumer life.

Recognizing obstacles to further growth, Sarnoff devised a plan to take the still fractured industry and stitch it together into a chain of stations to form the National Broadcasting Company. Thus, a program created in a New York studio could be piped simultaneously to stations in Texas, California, and Maine.

Along the way, and as early as 1927, scientists were developing the means to transmit a picture electronically through the air. Sarnoff's vision emerged once again as he saw television as the springboard to an entirely new form of broadcasting and the possibility of developing "theaters of the home."

When David Sarnoff died in 1971, the communications industry, which began as a start-up with wireless technology scarcely a century before, revolutionized human life and made an incredible impact on how people viewed the world.

The take-away lesson: Sarnoff's incredible success highlights, in part, paying constant attention to evolving consumer trends and then linking them to the applications of technology. Doing so does not depend on inspiration alone; rather a deliberate process is needed to formulate a credible strategic business plan. Then use the plan to sell the idea to another level of management — or to an outside source for funding. (See Chapter 8, 'Create an Effective Business Plan'.)

John H. Johnson, founder and owner of a complex of holdings including Ebony and Jet magazines and two cosmetics companies, exemplifies the grueling journey from a fragile start-up, through mountains of racial barriers, to a powerful industry leader. Johnson's success also demonstrates two components, which are ongoing themes of this book:

First, how a positive attitude, determination, courage, and ambition form the psychological mindset a manager needs to achieve any level of success.

Second, how to use the power of segmentation to maximize the impact of an organization's resources and successfully challenge industry leaders.

Long before experts spoke about the wonders of niche marketing, Johnson recognized the economic potential of the black American market. During the 1940s, 50s, and 60s, that market was largely ignored by the mainstream companies.

Yet with unshakeable confidence, Johnson moved forward to begin his first publication, *Negro Digest,* in 1942 at age 24. That publication and the follow-on magazines adhered to its founding mission statement "that expressed the brighter side of Negro life and highlighted Negro achievement."

The 1940s were also times of immense racial barriers where banks would not give business loans to blacks, and many office buildings would avoid renting space for the same reason. It was a time, too, when one of Johnson's key distributors would not handle his magazines, "because colored books don't sell."

In the end, however, distribution and the other stumbling blocks were overcome through a combination of dogged determination and sheer guts. He also singled out the top decision-makers in each industry and sold them through fact-based persuasion about the profit potential of the Negro market.

Johnson continued to move forward. Whereas his first magazine, *Negro Digest*, was modeled after *Reader's Digest*, his next magazine, *Ebony*, was developed in the image of the then hugely successful *Life* magazine. It was at that pivotal point a major issue surfaced.

The magazines needed a substantial amount of advertising to survive and prosper. "My problem was not circulation. My problem was advertising or, to come right out with it, the lack of advertising," declared Johnson.

During those early years, just as blacks were largely prohibited from conducting business with white companies, so it was that white advertisers did not buy space in black magazines. The legal and social segregation of mid-century America made it exceedingly difficult to do what was naturally open to other businesses.

Ambition, courage, and tenacity once again surfaced. Or as expressed by Johnson: "When I see a barrier, I cry and I curse, and then I get a ladder and climb over it."

And climb he did through a series of bold actions. Johnson began calling on executives from various companies and advertising agencies selling the idea that their advertising dollars would be well spent in *Ebony*. His confidence and tenacious efforts started to deliver results. By early 1948 he enlisted the likes of Zenith, Pepsi-Cola, Colgate, Beech-Nut, Seagram, and Remington Rand as advertisers for the magazine.

By 1983, it was estimated that Johnson's magazines reached nearly half the U.S. adult black population. He also became the first black man to land on the *Forbes* 400 list.

The take-away lesson: Barriers of all sizes and dimensions are natural parts of competitive life, especially in periods of severe economic difficulties. Overcoming any barriers begins and ends with the overall attitude and mindset of the individual. (See Chapter 2, 'Develop a Positive Mindset and Attitude'.)

Mary Kay, founder of **Mary Kay Cosmetics**, launched a direct-sales cosmetics company in 1963 when she was 45-years-old. It was also a time when most American women did not hold full-time jobs.

From a modest beginning at a small Dallas storefront, the start-up evolved in just 13 years to become the first company chaired by a woman to be listed on the New York Stock Exchange.

Mary Kay's success is based on sound business practices combined with tenacity and original thinking about the marketplace and about women themselves. She pieced together a corporate culture centered on education, participation, and empowerment of women. "I wasn't interested in the dollars-and-cents part of business; my interest in 1963 was in offering women opportunities that didn't exist anywhere else," she wrote later.

The result – An entrepreneurial culture emerged that inspired hundreds of thousands of Mary Kay saleswomen to become, in effect, small-business operators. That approach consisted of a homespun management style whereby Mary Kay boosted their self-esteem and confidence through constant positive reinforcement and material reward.

Mary Kay was introduced to direct selling in the 1930s selling children's books in her local community. Later she moved to a direct-sales housewares company where she excelled as a salesperson and as a manager of dozens of other salespeople. It was also a period when, of necessity, she supported herself and three children as a single mother.

Hoping for greater challenge and promotion, Mary Kay then moved on to another firm. It was not to happen; any promotion possibilities were clearly marked: Men only. She quit the company.

After a serious bout with depression, Mary Kay emerged with an idea and a detailed business plan for starting her own direct-sales company. First and foremost, the primary focus of the new company would be women. And it would have as its underpinnings the tough lessons of her prior experiences as a sole breadwinner for her family and the anxieties associated with working in male-oriented corporate cultures. To that end, Mary Kay developed a business model, which offered flexibility to part-time workers and allowed women to maintain their commitments to family while earning extra cash.

Scraping together start-up capital of $5,000, Mary Kay acquired a small inventory. Then she went about recruiting a sales force, known as consultants. Her business model called for consultants paying 50% of the retail price up-front for the cosmetics. This approach helped maintain ongoing cash flow to fund business growth. In effect, she operated a cash-and-carry system with no account receivables.

Starting with a facial cream she had known about from her previous company, Mary Kay secured the product by purchasing the original formula from its owner. She then went on to fill-out the product line with other skin care cosmetics.

Early on, a new hurdle surfaced: She found her product line-up went head-on against an industry leader, Avon. Still determined and not intimidated by the giant competitor, Mary Kay scrutinized Avon's operations and spotted two glaring weaknesses:

- First, the competitor did not concentrate on skin care, which turned out to be an advantage since that was Mary Kay's point of concentration and where she had outstanding products.
- Second, she concluded that Avon's door-to-door approach was, in her opinion, a dated sales method.

Pushing on, more consultants were added, which eventually pyramided into thousands. As the business prospered, Mary Kay created annual celebrations highlighted with awards to consultants who produced outstanding sales results. Mary Kay's "Ladder of Success" had rungs beginning with ribbons, bracelets, and reached to the highest level of the ladder, the coveted pink Cadillacs.

The personal and gracious touch by Mary Kay toward her people shaped the culture of the organization. Acting as a surrogate mother, for instance, she sent personally addressed birthday cards to thousands of consultants and called to inquire after sick family members.

The company continued to grow, notwithstanding a period of decline in the 1980s and 1990s when women began entering the business world and the professions in greater numbers. Mary Kay countered the decline by branching out to international markets, which launched a new spurt of growth as the company moved into Russia, Japan, and 21 other countries.

The take-away lesson: The Mary Kay case touches on four key points:

1. Business plans and strategies should be aligned with the core values of the organization, as expressed in its corporate culture. (See Chapter 3 and references to corporate culture in this chapter.)
2. To provide an historical base and a broader perspective for decision-making, study business methods from other industries and companies and then benchmark the best practices. (All chapters.)
3. Competitive intelligence is vitally important in shaping strategies and looking for weaknesses in the market leader. (See Chapter 5.)
4. There is no substitute for honing a solid skill in understanding the principles and techniques for developing competitive strategies. (See Chapter 4.)

The above examples — all start-ups — show how individuals overcame extraordinary odds and became remarkable successes. Given below, are more examples of others fitting that category:

David Ogilvy, who arrived from England, founded the advertising agency, Ogilvy & Mather. It quickly grew into one of the world's largest advertising firms. Ogilvy's theories helped change the face of advertising, many of which are still in practice today.

Ray Kroc, a 52-year-old milkshake machine salesman saw a hamburger stand in San Bernardino, California, and envisioned a massive new industry – fast food. As founder and builder, he revolutionized the American restaurant industry and created McDonald's Corporation, which would become a worldwide phenomenon.

Joseph Wilson headed **Haloid**, a small manufacturer of photographic papers, with minimal earnings and few employees. He developed a plan to create a whole new industry, which at the time seemed wildly optimistic. In fact, virtually no one predicted the staggering success that the company, renamed Xerox in 1961, would achieve. Not even Joseph Wilson.

Robert Noyce and **Gordon Moore** established **Intel** in 1968. They left the security of a large, established firm to start their own company. Their plan was to manufacture a product they had not yet invented – a tiny semiconductor chip with the same capacity to store computer memory as the large magnetic cores used in mainframe computers. The chip, called the microprocessor, is often ranked with McCormick's Reaper and Henry Ford's assembly line as a milestone in the history of invention.

BUSINESS-BUILDING OPPORTUNITIES TO OUTTHINK, OUTMANEUVER, AND OUTPERFORM YOUR COMPETITORS

Using the above case examples as a platform to trigger your thinking about company growth, you can integrate the following expandable ideas to create innovative opportunities.

Divided into Part One and Part Two, the 22 management ideas are grounded in solid experiences, with applications to a wide range of businesses.[1]

1. Many of the management ideas will be discussed in greater detail in the chapters that follow.

PART ONE

Set Up an Interactive Organization

Start by forming strategy teams consisting of individuals from different functional parts of your firm. Doing so serves two primary purposes:

First, teams fit precisely with one of the essential definitions of marketing management, which is a "total system of interacting business activities designed to plan, price, promote, and distribute want-satisfying products and services to consumers and business-to-business users in a competitive environment, at a profit."

Second, involving personnel from the functional areas of the business can refresh your thinking with potentially valuable insights, experiences, and solutions. Also, where they actively participate, you improve your chance of obtaining their buy-in on any plans they develop.

Therefore, it is in your best interest to engage individuals from various areas of your business into an interactive mode. Doing so ultimately improves the chances of exploiting new opportunities.

> ***Key point:***
>
> Form strategy teams and obtain valuable input from personnel who will implement your plan.

Develop Measurements

Sales, profits, return on investment, and other financials are well-established points for measurement. Yet, there are some objectives that you cannot easily quantify with metrics. And what you do measure in those areas reflects what happened in the past year, or in the past quarter. That is, they are historical, much like looking in a rearview mirror.

On the other hand, look at the ones you cannot quantify. For instance, most business plans contain a mission statement and a group of future-directed objectives yet to be realized. These may or may not have numbers associated with them; yet, they require some type of identifiable outcomes to keep you on course.

Some of those objectives include: Customer satisfaction levels, customer retention rates, corporate image, flexibility to react with speed to an emerging market trend, degree of preparedness against aggressive competitors, employee morale, customer relationships, operational efficiencies, effectiveness of internal communications, progress on innovation, and more.

The essential point: In situations where you are unable to come up with hard-nosed quantitative measures, create qualitative outcomes that are meaningful to you. Then you can gain an all-around view of your business, which introduces a balanced assessment beyond the standard financial numbers. In the process, you can "red flag" any underlying causes of an internal procedure or a market event, thereby getting an early-warning signal to make rapid adjustments.

Utilize Benchmarking

Benchmarking is an additional form of measurement, but serves a different purpose. The difference here is that you look to other industries and companies that excel in specific areas. It can apply to anything from production rates and defect levels to how you answer an inquiry.

First popularized in the 1970s by Xerox, benchmarking assesses your own performance and compares it with others, and if they are superior it helps you find out what it takes to match or exceed that level. This form of comparison broadens your perspective as you gain insight into how other companies operate. It thereby becomes not only a benchmark for your operation, it also stimulates fresh thinking and new ideas that can be adapted to give your operation a competitive advantage.

For a small company with limited resources and personnel, the best approach is to be somewhat selective about an area to benchmark. Therefore, select some function that is a key issue for you. It could be marketing, sales techniques, customer service, product design, distribution, or use of the Internet. Then, find the best company to benchmark against.

After comparison, judiciously adapt the most applicable approaches or techniques to improve your operation. The one caution: make sure what you pick-up fits with the operating culture of your organization and the marketplace in which you function.

> ***Key point:***
>
> Use benchmarking to broaden your perspective about how outstanding companies operate.

Focus on Innovation

The current management imperative among businesses seeking to survive and grow is to innovate — and keep innovating. This idea is anchored to the notion that you just don't confront competitors with me-too products and services, which equates with a direct frontal attack and results in profit-draining outcomes, such as commoditized products and price wars. Nor is innovation limited to just cutting-edge technology.

Rather, the focus on innovation is to take an indirect approach and bypass rivals with innovative products, services, and applications. To the extent that you can, you are trying to develop uniqueness for your firm. You are attempting to avoid replicating the strategies of yesterday in an operating environment that may not exist today.

Further, innovation reaches for unserved, neglected, and evolving market segments. So that, even segmentation goes beyond the traditional approaches and uses innovative ways to look at market segments, whereby you interface with your customers and create a new set of values for the buyer. (See Chapter 7.)

While it is not realistic to think that you can eliminate competition altogether, it is certainly possible to reduce the level of combative confrontations with rivals by using innovative approaches in key areas of your business.

> ***Key point:***
>
> Avoid repeating the strategies of yesterday and focus on innovative strategies.

Use Reengineering

Business process reengineering (BPR) was the hot management idea of the 1990s. But with the quest for cost control, quality, efficiencies, deploying resources for maximum effect, the concept is alive and well and takes on a second life, particularly for the small firm. The essence of the idea created by Michael Hammer and James Champy in their book, *Reengineering The Corporation*, is "don't automate, obliterate."

Their thesis was that instead of automating work that did not add value, companies should get rid of it. Fundamentally, you should take the same line of thinking and ask, "Why do we do this?" And "why do we do it this way?"

That means, you have to question the old rules and assumptions. So that reengineering doesn't stand for tweaking an existing procedure; it seeks to make substantial improvements.

Whereas the original application of BPR was geared to large organizations and focused primarily on backroom transactional processes, the current usage has a much broader scope, encompassing creative work ranging from product development to marketing.

> ***Key point:***
>
> Business Process Reengineering should question the old rules and assumptions and make appropriate improvements.

Establish a Brand

Tough to accomplish and costly to implement, especially for the small company, branding is generally accepted as a pinnacle of marketing success. One generally accepted definition says that branding is "the sum of all experiences and values associated with a particular product, service, or company," which goes beyond the original "name, mark, or symbol."

Branding attempts to humanize the product into a memorable set of experiences. While the known brands, such as Coca Cola, Kellogg's, and Campbell's Soup, as well as personalities like Madonna and Martha Stewart are widely known, branding can still be a viable strategy for a small company, especially if you operate in a limited market space and among a core group of customers.

Brands generally have commanded premium prices, too. However, that condition has not held up under all economic conditions. The recession period of 2007–2010 had a reverse effect, where unbranded generic products at lesser prices reversed the sales of some brands.

Notwithstanding, developing a brand image is a highly desirable strategy in situations where you try to value your product with such attributes as reliability, quality, or service. It is all part of distinguishing your product from competitors by fixing those favorable features in your customers' minds.

There is still another benefit: brand extension. Here, you can extend the merits associated with the existing product into a new product (providing that brand name fits into the market segment you are going after.) You thereby take some risk out of a new product introduction.

Key point:

Branding attempts to humanize a product.

Manage Your Supply Chain

The supply chain is made up of the physical and information links between suppliers and the company on one side, and the company and its customers on the other. It takes in production planning, purchasing, materials handling and logistics, which includes transport, warehousing, and distribution centers.

The central idea is that you should view the supply chain as one continuous route so that an order reaches the customer complete, in the right place, undamaged, and on time. Where distribution was once considered a separate company function, the supply chain is now viewed as a competitive weapon. If you can handle the chain better than a rival, you are in a better position to obtain and retain the business.

Also, you will find efficient supply chain management is highly relevant for small companies seeking to avoid money-draining activities associated with maintaining high levels of inventory and costly warehousing. The marketing benefit also ties into the popular approach of just-in-time delivery.

Whereas there are many plusses to a well-run supply chain, it does depend on accurate sales forecasting and some computer systems. If you use outsourcing and long-distance transportation, it is critical that the numerous links in the chain operate smoothly.

Identify Your Core Competencies

Pioneered by authors Gary Hamel and C.K. Prahalad, core competence is something that you do better than anyone else. They laid down three tests to identify a core competence:

- It provides potential access to a wide variety of markets;
- It makes a significant contribution to perceived customer benefits of the end product;
- It is difficult to imitate.

While the concept is most associated with large organizations, it is certainly appropriate for the small firm, which is not usually encumbered with a complex organization and many business units. Looking for your core competence is well worth your time and effort; it feeds competitive advantage.[2]

> ***Key point:***
>
> Identify your core competency to gain a competitive advantage.

Sharpen Your Skills in Developing a Business Plan

The strategic business plan (Chapter 8) helps you explore ways to make your business unique. You are guided through a systematic process that most often generates fresh opportunities.

For instance, the first step in the plan is to develop a strategic direction. The approach opens your mind to look out in an orderly, timely, and far reaching manner, and envision what you want your business to look like in three to five years.

Next, you are asked to come up with objectives to give your strategic direction some concrete and measurable outcomes.

Then, you develop strategies. This is the defining moment in your planning. Strategies, defined here as actions to achieve the objectives, set in motion a whole range of activities that fulfill your vision for the firm. They guide your decisions, shape your product line, and define the scope of your activities. Next, you are guided to the grassroots tactics that you will employ to acquire customers and fight-off competitors.

The strategic business plan is the single most important document you can develop. All functions of the business from production to marketing emanate from the plan.

In basic terms: The plan outlines how to get where you want to go. It also serves as a prime communicator to reach your employees and get them to embrace the plan.

---

2. Within the following chapters, you will find numerous checklists and guidelines to assist in meeting the above criteria. Also see the Strategy Diagnostic Tool in the last section of the book.

Planning can become quite complex with numerous consultants and others adding more procedures to follow, more analysis to undertake, and more measurements to record. It is in your best interest to avoid complexity and keep the plan simple and flexible.

Key point:

Avoid complexity; keep business plans simple and flexible.

Practice Customer Relationship Management (CRM)

Pure and simple, CRM means: concentrate on your customers, learn about their needs and behaviors, use what you learn to improve relationships and, ultimately, sell them more.

Perhaps the late management scholar Peter Drucker said it best decades ago: "The purpose of business is to create a customer."

After a considerable number of false starts, CRM software is becoming more reliable and affordable for the small firm. Through data warehousing and data mining programs, customers' lifestyles, buying habits, and estimates of their overall value to the business are being assembled. In turn, the data is converted into useable marketing information.

For instance, you can single out low-value customers to be shifted to low-cost channels such as telemarketing or the website, while high-value prospects are pinpointed for face-to-face contact. The data derived from a CRM program also permits opportunities to cross-sell or up-sell.

Key point:

CRM focuses on the customer – their needs and behaviors, improves relationships and leads to more sales.

Empower Your Personnel

Empowerment has been floating around for decades, along with its champions and critics. In the end, however, empowerment works. Where it doesn't work, it may not be fully applied, but is merely being given lip service.

That is, taking people's opinion about something is not the same as empowering them to make decisions about their jobs. Second-guessing decisions that you have just empowered someone to make doesn't feel enabling to the decision-maker.

The central idea, backed by credible studies, indicates that the perceptions an individual holds about the importance of his or her job, as well as its place in the organization's plans, had a bigger impact on loyalty and customer service than all other employee factors combined. Empowerment is clearly a function of leadership and management practice.

To the extent you are able, create an all-inclusive operating environment for empowerment to flourish. You thereby benefit from your people becoming more excited, more driven, more involved with their work. Becoming immersed in their jobs, they will cooperate not because they have to, but because they want to.

Big businesses have to make a major effort to initiate empowerment, whereas it is a natural pathway for the smaller company. Take advantage of it!

> ***Key point:***
>
> Create an all-inclusive work environment for empowerment to flourish.

Rediscover the Marketing Concept

Embedded in the marketing concept is the marketing mix, also known as the familiar 4Ps (product, price, promotion, place or distribution.) This classic model evolved from a production orientation, where managers concentrated on goods they could make most efficiently, at a cost that would create a market for them.

As competition increased, the sales concept emerged, where managers focused on where to sell the product. For the most part, customers did not play a primary role in managers' thinking.

Only after World War II did marketing in today's framework begin to evolve. Managers began to ask pointed questions: "What does the customer want?" "And can we produce it?"

It began the formal period of inquiring about customers' needs before the product was developed. Over time a more penetrating question was asked: "Do we have an outside-in orientation; or do we use an inside-out orientation?" That thinking gave birth to the marketing concept.

The 4Ps, now over 45-years-old, is still regarded as a highly valuable concept to latch on to. First, it encompasses the functional areas of the business, along with the input of those respective individuals. Second, it broadens your thinking to the numerous possibilities for creating opportunities and challenging competitors.

For achieving your purposes, make certain the marketing concept is embedded deeply in your operation and within you and your staff's thinking. It is the customer-first orientation that leads to market opportunities.

Key point:

Marketing Mix is still an important concept in today's environment and should be instilled in your operation and in staff's thinking.

Master the Internet

The beginnings of the Internet can be traced to the packet-switching and networking ideas at MIT in the early 1960s. Yet, it was not until the 1980s that business began to see the commercial possibilities. From there, the Internet evolved into websites for information.

However, it was in the more structured environment of business-to-business transactions that e-commerce began to gain momentum. As confidence grew in conducting transactions, consumers embraced the Web and it became an integral part of shopping and information.

Now considered part of the basic business infrastructure, the Internet is the means individuals and organizations use to conduct transactions, communicate data, collaborate to develop new knowledge, and express opinions through an expanding portfolio of social networks.

If you have not tapped the Internet yet, the opportunities are open for you to master the Internet and integrate it into your business.

> ***Key point:***
>
> The Internet is part of the basic infrastructure of a business and is essential in conducting certain major functions.

Develop Your Strategic Direction

Discussed earlier under business plans, strategic direction, also known as a mission statement or vision statement, permits you to look outward over an expanse of at least three to five years and ask, "What business am I in?" "What business should I be in?"

Those questions are attributed to Theodore Levitt, late professor at the Harvard Business School and his 1960 classic article, "Marketing Myopia" in the *Harvard Business Review.*

It isn't a fanciful exercise. Rather, those questions permit you to thoughtfully reexamine your business or product line in the light of your internal capabilities and resources. The application also helps you ponder new product ideas, look at available or emerging markets, appraise both domestic and foreign competitors, and more.

His approach began by pointing out that every major industry was once a growth industry. Some were into decline; others had already stopped growing. However, it was his example of the railroad industry, which gave "Marketing Myopia" fame and longevity.

Levitt wrote, "... railroads assumed themselves to be in the railroad business rather than in the transportation business. The reason they defined their industry incorrectly was that they were railroad-oriented instead of transportation-oriented; they were product-oriented instead of customer-oriented."

It is well worth your time to go through such an exercise with members of your staff, as you search for fresh opportunities and new growth. The process is presented in the chapter on business planning.

> ***Key point:***
>
> Strategic direction permits you to assess your business, capabilities, and resources. It helps you look forward at new ideas and markets.

PART TWO

This part focuses on leadership and strategy ideas, with links to Part One:

Stay on the Offensive

Boldness is desirable. Such an approach depends, however, on the availability of resources and the level of confidence you show in yourself and your employees. Whereas, boldness does have a measure of risk, think about the possible paralyzing effects that excessive caution could have on your business and its dismal consequences on the morale of your staff.

Boldness in this context doesn't endorse a shoot-from-the-hip impulsive act. It does suggest using the following introspective process:

- Define clear objectives, develop a strategy, calculate the resources needed to reach your goals, determine the possible response from competitors to your actions, monitor your markets and customers, and develop an exit strategy should it be needed. Once the process is completed, then implement the plan.

As for implementation: If you empowered your staff to undertake the plans and the bold action succeeds, offer ample rewards; if failure results, avoid damaging repercussions.

Key point:

Boldness wins over excessive caution.

Encourage Entrepreneurial Thinking

As with empowerment, seek maximum input from all levels of employees. Sort through new ideas that could lead to new products, evolving markets, or new businesses. Maintain a cultural sensibility that permits open mindness and avoids the idea-killing verbiage, "We've tried that."

Also allow sufficient time for ideas to incubate and hatch into new technologies, products, and services. Develop channels of communications that permit employees to submit ideas. If within your power, require them to submit *opportunity proposals* as part of their duties.

Such proposals should consist of products or markets that would create new revenue streams. Backed-up with the suitable research to show its feasibility, each proposal should show the rationale for expending valuable company resources. In turn, that translates into such metrics as sales, profits, share of market, as well as data on gaining a foothold in a new market segment.

As part of the arrangement, if you and other senior managers accept the proposal, then it is a shared responsibility for its success or failure. It is all about thinking and acting entrepreneurially.

Key point:

Open your mind to new ideas and encourage all levels of employees to contribute.

Learn to Live in a Flexible Competitive Environment

This is a cultural attribute that is often difficult to embed within an organization, and equally difficult to instill in employees. Living with the uncertainty of aggressive competitors calls for management's full support, especially during this period of severe market volatility.

As for your personal behavior, support means maintaining a visible display of resolute calmness and steadfast confidence. As for your employees, some may find extreme change creates an unsettling internal feeling, weighed down by apprehension and fear. Still, flexibility is a singular behavioral quality that must be upheld.

Some changes are in your hands to control. Others are issues outside of your ability to handle, such as the value of currencies, trade rules, and other legislative or environmental issues. Notwithstanding, some issues can result in prime opportunities or challenging barriers.

Still, agility is needed especially in a global economy with the rampant use of interactive communications, vibrant technology applications, and the still-evolving innovative use of the Internet. All of which sets in motion conditions that can swamp you or activate new opportunities.

Act as an Aggressive Competitor

The object here is to gain insight about the health of your organization and to determine if it can successfully fend off a competitor's intrusion.

One workable approach to examining your firm's ability to act as an aggressive competitor is to conduct the following training exercise. To begin, divide your participating personnel into two teams:

Team #1 represents your firm. The goal of Team #1 is to defend itself against an aggressive competitor and maintain its market position.

Team #2 acts as your primary competitor. Team # 2 plays the role of the forceful competitor with the aim of developing strategies that attack Team #1's position by exposing its weaknesses and disrupting its plans.

As a training exercise, it is an excellent approach to test long-held attitudes and assumptions by exposing strong points and areas of vulnerability.

The central idea: You discover where your firm has an advantage, or where it might languish at risk. By this means, you size-up strengths and limitations in your leadership, product line, technical and customer services, logistics, as well as your overall company makeup. You also get to look at relationships with suppliers, intermediaries, and customers along the entire supply chain.

Also, this exercise highlights the behavior of those managers who cannot make a determined effort to take-on an aggressive posture. Meaning: Not all individuals are effective at performing optimally through successive stages of a corporate cycle — start-up, growth, maturity, and decline — or even within different cultural environments.

As important, the process exposes strong points and areas of vulnerability, which might endanger your firm to competitive attacks. (The guidelines for conducting such a survey are provided in the chapters that follow.)

> ***Key point:***
>
> Discover where your firm has an advantage, or if it is in danger of languishing at risk.

Build a Solid Market Position

Your aim is to create a unique market position from which competitors cannot easily dislodge you. To the extent you are able, try to create areas that you can support with tangible claims. It is all part of mounting a long-term positive image for your firm.

There are two approaches you can take:

First, conduct an analysis by focusing on the components of the marketing mix. Also take a candid look at the capabilities and behavior of your people. Doing so gives you a fairly detailed assessment of areas in which they excel. It also highlights places where they are underperforming.

Second, take the following steps:

- Position yourself in the market so that the competitor cannot anticipate your moves quickly enough to counter your moves.
- Focus your resources on an emerging, neglected, or poorly served market. Your aim is to avoid a direct, head-on confrontation with a stronger rival.
- Create a differentiated product, or value-added service, that is not easily cloned.
- Develop a system that provides quick market feedback so that you can take remedial action against any negative factors in the marketplace.
- Initiate constructive relationships with customers that lock-out competitors for an extended sales cycle.

Stay Close to Evolving Technology

Immerse yourself in the technologies that can launch your business into new levels of performance. For instance, customer relationship management software lets you track your customers and markets.

Now you can obtain insights about what your customers want before designing a new product. Better yet, you can involve them in the developmental process, which lets your customers specify the key features they would like before a product is assembled.

Or look to the evolving use of cloud computing, which is a major shift in the way companies obtain software and computing capacity by tapping into Web-based applications.

Then, there is the current generation of software that offers even more efficient ways to gather information collected at companies'

Websites, direct response operations, customer service call centers, retail stores, and field sales.

Therefore, tuning in to what is happening in technologies can help you develop fresh opportunities. You have several choices open to you: buy or lease a technology, invest in start-up technology firms, or partner with a compatible company.

Key point:

Tune-in to technologies that can make a vital difference in taking advantage of an opportunity.

Watch Psychological Influences

Emotions surface as positive motivators or inhibiting barriers. They can span the extremes of behavior, such as: optimism vs. defeatism, boldness vs. faint-heartedness, compliant vs. insubordinate, decisive vs. vacillating, involved vs. laid-back, spirited vs. worrying, stable vs. confused, enthusiastic vs. discouraged.

These humanist expressions by your staff can either expand into sparks of positive outcomes or fall into chasms of unrealized opportunities. They have consequences for the total organization or an individual business unit and can certainly impact your plans in one direction or another.

Therefore, it is in your best interest to become deeply aware of the psychological influences that are playing out in your operation. By adding the human touch, you attempt to reach the hearts and minds of your personnel. In so doing, you draw on their innate capabilities, which energizes their involvement and potentially creates unrealized levels of creativity. (See following chapter.)

The essential point: Even if you develop the optimum business plan, it is of little or no value unless your people willingly activate it. They can do so with your eager support.

> ***Key point:***
>
> Be attentive to your staff's emotions, which in turn will motivate and energize them to be creative and perform.

Develop a Healthy Corporate Culture

Allied to psychological influences is the grassroots culture of your company, which takes into account the history, values, behavioral patterns, and ideas that sets your firm apart from others.

Culture encapsulates the soul of an organization. It defines your organization's DNA. It highlights the principles for which it stands. Unfortunately, culture is still an often-overlooked factor in galvanizing individuals into action and asserting leadership. Yet it is pivotal to the vitality and ultimately the successful outcome of any business effort.

Even with a superficial observation of how your company reacts in a variety of competitive situations, you should be able to determine if the behaviors and attitudes of individuals are equal to the task when played out in the realism of a hard-hitting global economy. Will they be proactive or passive; confident or worried; daring or timid?

Depending on what you observe, is there an identifiable set of historical values, or a collection of intrinsic beliefs by which you can rally individuals and energize them to act with conviction and thereby change an adverse situation into a positive one?

In a different time period and another organizational setting, U.S. Civil War General William T. Sherman observed, "There is a soul to an army as well as to the individual man. And no general can accomplish the full work of his army unless he commands the soul of his men, as well as their bodies and legs."

The end game is: Corporate culture must be aligned with the strategic goals of your business plan. This vital correlation determines which objectives can, and cannot, be realistically achieved. Doing so closes any gaps that exist between your aspirations to develop opportunities and your ability to execute a plan.

Key point:

Align your corporate culture with the goals of your business plan.

Summarizing: You can employ all of the above ideas to drive change and energize your company. How drastic those changes are depends on the severity of your company's problems. Therefore, you can react to problems as they arise; or you can be proactive by anticipating changes.

It is all part of leadership and managerial competence, which relies heavily on estimating your internal and external environments, including competitors, suppliers and, most of all, your customers.

Now, let's move on to Chapter 2, which shows you how to create opportunities by developing a positive mindset and attitude.

2

Develop a Positive Mindset and Attitude

Apple unveils an iPod Shuffle half the size of its previous model, but able to play twice as many songs.

Wal-Mart sells a package to doctors for electronic medical records through its Sam's Clubs.

Charles Schwab provides a one-year, no-fee consultation service to select clients.

Yahoo launches three new products designed to help marketers deliver more relevant display ads tied to user search behavior.

What do the above company examples have in common?

First, they all launched a new product or service during a severe recession and intense global competition.

Second, they all made use of a powerful driving force, the human element, which became the foundation of all their energetic activities. That is, all actions that preceded and followed the introductions were handled by individuals with a positive mindset.

Those individuals proved responsive to fresh ideas, innovative about developing business-building strategies, and enthusiastic when implementing their plans. They succeeded in their actions in spite of harsh competitive conditions.

In contrast, a more cautious and typical reaction would dictate that during difficult economic times the best approach would be to trigger a variety of cost-saving plans, such as, halt new product introductions, shelve costly projects, reduce marketing expenditures, examine every activity for maximum pay-out, and the ultimate step, lay-off personnel.

Initiating survival strategies in a tough economy is one thing, and quite acceptable, where few new ideas materialize, or where managers and staff are immobilized by excessive fear and caution. Nevertheless, it's no great comfort when you consider that growing a business is the true measure of a company's long-term progress. Retreating is not what you bargained for.

So what about the human element, identified by an individual's attitude, state of mind, and overall way of thinking? You can compare the mind to a deep pool of possibilities set in motion by thoughts that reflect intuitive insights. These can be positive or negative, depending on the input of the controlling beliefs.

In turn, the output shapes an individual's core behavior. On the positive side, insights can lead to innovative thinking that translates to competitive advantage and bold new opportunities, as in the above examples.

On the negative side, insights bolted to fear produce pessimistic attitudes that can strangle creativity, shut down ideas, and blind the individual to problem-solving possibilities.

To assist you in taking a broad look at behavior and the possibilities of changing mindsets and attitudes, consider the following guidelines. In addition to reviewing your own behavior, they are meant to assess your employees' behavior.

The aim: Inspire those who are generally positive and compliant, the not-so-compliant, individuals with negative feelings, and even persons with insubordinate behavior.

Key point:

The human mind is likened to a deep pool of possibilities triggered by thoughts and attitudes.

From a managerial viewpoint, the purpose of the review is to bind your employees' hearts and minds to positive actions when they face the inevitable competitive battles that lie ahead.

Action Steps

1. *Take the time to expand your employees' views of what is going on beyond their limited access to information.*

Your initial approach is to bring your employees to a point of living in-tune with their surroundings. Specifically, get them to reach a state of awareness.

Awareness, in this framework, takes into account the following issues: how competitors' actions can disrupt your plans, how to interpret market events and their impact on your strategies, and how to draw correct conclusions from market intelligence to create new opportunities.

Therefore, your purpose is to get your employees to look outside their four walls and understand the wider competitive world. Through on-line communications, face-to-face informal meetings, weekly or monthly briefings, update your staff about markets, industries, and competitive conditions.

These get-togethers serve several purposes, among them:

- You recognize the value of providing your staff with the above information.
- You motivate them by providing a venue so they can participate with fresh insights.
- You tap their diversity, thought patterns, experiences, and collective knowledge, thereby integrating individuals and their functions.
- You obtain viewpoints that can provide useful perspectives and constructive comparisons.
- You bring unity to your group.

The major outcome: Get your employees to internalize that you and they walk together on a very narrow path, which includes numerous visible and unseen obstacles. The most important issue is not to be afraid. That is, if there is a balance of a positive mindset linked with an objective interpretation of market events, success is overweighted in your favor.

Increasingly, a wide variety of communications vehicles permit you to take the high road and initiate programs and exchanges of information. Such is the case with the mushrooming use of social networks, blogs, e-mail, instant messaging, video conferencing, corporate wikis, and the like. Also, face time, thought to be outmoded by electronic communications, is still prevalent and noticeably on the increase.

With smaller companies spreading into global markets, and where there is a heightened diversity in the workforce, the need to unite individuals to a common goal intensifies. Reason: Individuals tend to be wherever their thoughts are. You want to make certain their thoughts as well as your own, from a business viewpoint, are where you would like them to be.

Therefore, stay close to your employees, so that you can sensitize yourself to their thoughts, moods, temperaments, and increasingly the nuances of their local cultures. All the while, your aim is to integrate them into the mainstream of your company's goals.

Doing so also allows you to focus individuals' attention on constructive projects that can take even a sketchy idea and convert it into a new product or service. The exciting possibility exists for an embryonic innovation to sprout into new revenue streams.

Key point:

Stay close to your employees, so that you can sensitize yourself to their thoughts, moods, temperaments, and local cultures.

Otherwise, without some guidance their creative thoughts would radiate like sunbeams. At first, they seem solid until you try to grasp them. You thereby lose the potential value of huge business-building resources.

Thus, reach out to the special needs of your employees and focus on sustaining their psychological well-being. As a result, you should see tangible improvement in performance, innovation, and employee harmony.

2. *Recognize that many employees harbor ingrained habits, which are often inclined toward negative feelings, fears, and a lack of confidence.*

There is substantial harm to employee morale if negative habits are left unattended. Make every effort to break those habits. Do all you can to convince them not to make the same mistake as others who prematurely give up trying to change because they feel stuck in their behavior.

Demonstrate to them that if they truly want to, and are willing to work hard enough, they can overcome negative habits. Here is where discipline plays a positive role. In effect, it's a test designed for them to exercise freedom of choice. The issue, then, is for them to choose wisely.

Your best approach is to set up (or recommend) a program to deal with negativity. Where possible, utilize outside specialists. Specify a clear-cut objective to help individuals resist negative thoughts. Often, they can direct the process to clear the blockages that prevent implementing your business plan. (See Table 2.1.)

Table 2.1. Areas in Which Behavioral Specialists Provide Assistance

- Conduct individual and group coaching
- Analyze and advise on complex personnel issues related to inner feelings and external behavior
- Conduct needs assessments to define training objectives; also match the right person to the right job
- Communicate company vision, objectives, and cultural values
- Monitor the workforce during the development of business plans and competitive strategies
- Perform damage control due to employee performance rising out of difficult competitive conditions

By taking such positive action to harness your human capital, you acknowledge that your people are a major influence in market performance. And, as important, they function as a key competitive differentiator.

In sum, whereas the profit motive normally drives major decisions, the more urgent considerations for you, and the intentions of this book, are the behavioral issues natural to your personnel.

3. *Learn to wait.*

As noted above, maintain continuing dialogue with your staff so that you can become aware of the direction of their thinking and mindset. In particular, such insight is significant should you have to delay your plans due to sudden market events.

In that case, you are likely to find a heightened level of anxiety not only within yourself, but with your staff. This is where you, and they, must cool down and wait for better timing. This is the moment, despite all determined efforts, to learn disciplined patience.

The essential point: Between acceptance and anxiety, choose acceptance, with the proviso that patience is only a pause, nothing more, that allows you time to reignite your efforts with fresh ideas and innovative strategies.

4. *Learn to restrain irritation.*

Help your people avoid being provoked by negative surroundings. This means creating compatible relationships with others. Does this imply that you have to assume the role of an active mediator? For the most part the answer is a resounding yes.

Yet some managers will back-off and ask the opposing groups to work through their problems. Notwithstanding, it is your obligation that once anger, frustration, and continuing dispute move forward beyond a reasonable time, you have to take an active role in setting a pathway for conflict resolution.

Still other executives intentionally create opposition in their ranks, thinking that it leads to a healthy work environment. However, it is with a degree of risk, when compared to the far greater benefit of creating harmony and unity of effort.

Nonetheless, strained relationships do exist among various functional areas of an organization, such as marketing vs. finance, product development vs. distribution, manufacturing vs. sales, and so on.

> ***Key point:***
>
> Once anger, frustration, and dispute move beyond a reasonable time, take an active role in setting a pathway for conflict resolution.

For the most part, however, hostilities are counterproductive, especially when flaring anger dominates the scene. Clashing groups seldom arrive at an acceptable solution. Within such a fractured situation, your aim is to promote workable outcomes based on internal operating conditions, the dynamics of the marketplace, and the activities of competitors.

Then, you are more likely to come to a peaceful and healing condition among all parties — even where groups live as opposites, but not opponents. It takes a measure of sensitive awareness on your part. For it is easy to criticize others and make them feel unwanted. Any manager can do that. What takes effort and leadership skill is raising them up and making them feel good.

5. *Learn to look for the good in yourself and your employees.*

Avoid the unnecessary search for shortcomings and weak points in yourself and employees, unless there is a deliberate effort to conduct a needs analysis for future training. Focus on their good attributes. Highlight them and turn even indifferent employees into winners.

Keep in mind, too, they are the ones who will carry out your plan, which has at stake your personal reputation — and perhaps your job.

In the process, be alert for the inevitable expressions of hardship, complaints of tough work, and sacrifices that often surface among workers during any emergency. Distinguish between what you would consider grueling work, however, and merely a display of whining and grumbling. To counter any emotionally charged outbursts, indicate to the rest of the staff the consequences if they continue with their flare-ups.

If you succeed in choking-off their complaints, and as a result of their sacrifices and hard work, you show first-rate results, point out that those positive results are only the beginnings of other good outcomes.

It is your opportunity to say, "If you call this good, I'll really show you what good is. I'll show you how this company can grow and how each of you can benefit financially and professionally." Of course, this approach must be anchored to tangible and realistic assessments that the staff can understand, believe in, and rally around.

What ties into that approach are the opportunities that emerge each day. Some are quite apparent, others require more searching. Also, what might appear as sameness could be an opportunity under a different set of market conditions.

As long as there is a mindset tuned to fresh opportunities, it is your job to instill in your people the ability to seek possibilities out of what every day and each event has to offer.

You and your employees must see the point of change, agree with it, and be of the same opinion about altering behavior.

Social psychologist Leon Festinger published his famous theory of cognitive dissonance, which is the distressing mental state that arises when people find that their beliefs are inconsistent with their actions. Consequently, there is a deepseated need to eliminate cognitive dissonance by changing either your employees' actions or their beliefs.

Workers will be happy to change their individual behavior if they understand why and how their actions contribute to the overall company's fortunes. Also, they will act positively if they believe it is personally worthwhile for them to play an active role in the organization. (Look again at Action step 1.)

As part of the change, utilize a workable system of rewards and recognition. Using incentives have a scientific foundation, which is based on B.F. Skinner's[1] theories of conditioning and positive reinforcement, as well as the classic motivational behavior concepts of Herzberg, McGregor, Maslow, and Ouchi. (See Table 2.2.)

Table 2.2. Motivational Behavior

Herzberg's Motivation-Hygiene Theory

The most important part of Herzberg's theory is that the main motivating factors are embedded in the satisfaction gained from the job itself.

He reasoned that to motivate an individual, a job must be challenging with sufficient scope for enrichment and interest. Motivators-often called satisfiers-are directly concerned with the satisfactions gained from a job.

In contrast, a lack of motivators lead to over-concentration on what Herzberg called hygiene factors-or dissatisfiers-which form the basis for complaints.

The top six factors causing dissatisfaction and satisfaction consist of:

Factors leading to dissatisfaction	Factors leading to satisfaction
1. Organizational policy	1. Sense of achievement
2. Quality of management	2. Level of recognition
3. Relationship with boss	3. Intrinsic value of the job
4. Working conditions	4. Level of responsibility
5. Wages	5. Opportunities for advancement
6. Interpersonal relationships	6. Status provided

McGregor's X Y Theory

This theory still remains a valid and predictable means by which you can develop a positive leadership style. It is central to organizational development and corporate culture.

McGregor maintained that there are two fundamental approaches to managing people: Popularized as Theory X and Theory Y.

Theory X tends to use an authoritarian leadership style. In contrast, Theory Y leans toward a participative approach. In today's environment, Theory Y generally is accepted as producing better performance, in that it allows people more latitude to grow and develop in self-motivating surroundings.

The two styles are contrasted as follows:

1. B.F. Skinner is listed as the most influential psychologist of the 20th century. He was a prolific author who published 21 books and 180 articles.

Theory X (Authoritarian Management Style)	Theory Y (Participative Management Style)
• The average person dislikes work and will avoid it, if possible. • People must be forced to work towards organizational objectives. • Individuals prefer to be directed, look to avoid responsibility, generally lack ambition, and want security above all else.	• Effort in work is natural and enjoyable. • People will apply self-control and self-direction in the pursuit of organizational objectives, without external control, or the threat of punishment. • Commitment to objectives is a function of rewards associated with their achievement. • People usually accept and often seek responsibility. • People use a high degree of imagination, ingenuity, and creativity to solve business problems.

Maslow's Hierarchy of Needs

Maslow viewed people as basically trustworthy, self-protecting, and self-governing. Further, he believed that individuals' innate tendencies are toward growth.

According to Maslow's theory, there are five types of needs that must be satisfied before a person can act unselfishly. These needs are arranged in rank order and usually shown as a pyramid.

The path is to satisfy one set of needs at a time, beginning with the physiological need, then move upward to self-actualization.

Maslow's Hierarchy of Needs:

5. Self-Actualization
4. Esteem
3. Belonging
2. Safety
1. Physiological Needs

Physiological needs:

These cover the basic functions of comfort and maintenance of the body, such as: food, drink, heat, shelter, sleep, and health.

Safety needs:

These refer not just to physical safety and protection from harm, but to such areas as financial security, employment, medical and legal assistance, and all means that maintain stability.

Belonging needs:

These indicate the need for human contact: family, friends, relationships, teams, and general contact in society.

Esteem needs:

These recognize the need for status, power, prestige, acknowledgement, respect, and responsibility. Such requirements provide individuals with a higher position within a group.

Self-actualization needs:

After all the previous needs have been satisfied, the top of the pyramid deals with the individual's need to reach for his or her full potential and strive for individual destiny.

Ouchi's Theory Z

This theory is essentially a combination of all that is best about McGregor's Theory Y and modern Japanese management. It places a large amount of freedom and trust in workers. It also assumes that they possess strong loyalty and interest in teamwork and the organization.

Theory Z places a great deal of reliance on the attitudes and responsibilities of workers, whereas McGregor's X Y theory is mainly focused on management and motivation from the manager's and organization's perspective.

What follows is a set of conditions common to whichever style you adopt:

- Hold fast to the definitive object of all business, which according to the late management scholar, Peter Drucker, is to "create a customer."
- Remove obstacles that deprive people from gaining pride in quality of service and delivering innovative products.
- Breakdown inhibiting barriers among diverse staffs and create collaborative cross-functional teams.
- Introduce a work environment where the emphasis is on managers leading, not merely supervising.
- Commit to long-term goals, such as attaining market leadership, developing leading-edge products, or maintaining superior service and product quality.
- Eliminate the use of fear as a motivator.
- Encourage employees to express ideas; listen to them and respond.
- Promote self-improvement as an ongoing imperative. Institute continuing employee training and education to advance their skills, personal growth, and chances for career advancement.

As part of motivational behavior, you have to install reporting procedures to set targets, measure performance, and hand-out rewards. These measures must be consistent with the tasks you ask your staff to take on, which includes making certain they have the skills and knowledge to do the job.

As part of the process, your employees must see you in action. That means they should look to you as a role model, even to the point of copying your behavior. Therefore, remain highly visible. Your staff needs to see you at work and gain confidence in your decisions.

Key point:

Employees must see you in action. Remain highly visible.

The former CEO of **General Electric**, Jack Welch, fits such a role.

In 19 years, during which time many company executives failed in an uncompromising global economy, the much-celebrated chief executive led GE to one revenue and earnings record after another.

He devoted more than half his time to people issues. With his informal face-to-face leadership style, he gained the steadfast respect of his employees. He acted as if each employee with whom he made contact was a friend and associate.

As he casually wandered down aisles to check the stacked products, every employee from clerk to factory worker knew him as Jack. His favorite practice was to bypass the corporate hierarchy and communicate directly up, down, and across layers of management.

His handwritten notes, sent to everyone from direct reports to hourly workers, presented a lasting, and in some cases, an emotional impression. All those actions were intended to lead, guide, and influence the behavior of individuals throughout GE's complex organization.

Lessons emerge from the GE example for the smaller firm: You want to keep a pattern of consistency throughout your company. You must make certain that you and other managers agree on the direction of the company, ways of working, and paths to follow in seeking opportunities.

Along the same lines, where entrepreneurial decision-making is encouraged at lower levels, coach junior employees on how to spot fresh opportunities. One approach is to provide broad guidelines and leave the actual search up to the employees.

The essential points: (1) activate a principle of entrepreneurial thinking and (2) encourage subordinates to look critically for new opportunities.

For instance, guidelines for seeking opportunities would include the following two categories:

Revenue-expansion opportunities:

- What opportunities are there to reduce customers'[2] returns and complaints?
- What processes would speed-up production and delivery to benefit customers?
- How can we improve customers' market position and image?
- How would investing in greater brand identity impact customers' revenues, as well as our own?
- What product or service technologies would enhance customers' operations?
- How can we create differentiation that offers customers a competitive advantage?
- How would improving re-ordering procedures impact revenues?

Cost-reduction opportunities:

- What possibilities are there to cut customers' purchasing costs?

2. In this listing, customers are defined as middle men or distributors. You'll also find that several of the points apply to consumers or end-users, as well.

- What processes would reduce customers' production costs?
- What systems or technologies would decrease customers' production downtime?
- What approaches would slash customers' delivery costs?
- What methods would trim customers' administrative overheads?
- What strategies would maximize customers' working capital?

Where possible, involve as many of your people in the above process, especially those who can actively think about such areas as customers' needs, market growth, and competitive advantage.

Here are practical approaches:

Get others involved – from managers to experienced sales people – who would serve as positive contributors. Have them brief the group about the benefits of paying attention to market-driven opportunities.

Then, show them the potential impact on the company, as well as the contributions to their personal career growth. If necessary, focus on information briefings to instill the appropriate attitudes. Also, to encourage a mindset that is positive, outward looking, and progressive, turn to thoughts, words, and initiatives, which could trigger positive ideas and entrepreneurial thinking.

As for the words you use: Nothing exists without meaning. Nothing subsists independently. What you say and how you communicate can serve as spiritual, energizing, or conceptual thoughts.

While you would like the words and uplifting thoughts to be your own, where appropriate use meaningful quotes of others. These help persuade and motivate your people to action. And to a great measure, they would add authenticity to the message you are trying to get across.

Minimally use words that reach the heart of those you manage and you will be rewarded with attitudes that can overcome your greatest obstacles. In like manner, listen to your employees, share their concerns, address any doubts they might be harboring.

In the end, without energy words, plans have little chance of being implemented successfully. And when words are carefully orchestrated and controlled, the end result is remarkable. What you want to create is a state of mind where despair does not exist.

Key point:

Without energy words, plans have little chance of being implemented successfully. And when words are orchestrated and controlled, the end result is remarkable.

Yet, even in your desire to have your people act with positive attitudes, the reality of human behavior is that negative thoughts do prevail. Such thoughts shape an alarming mindset of losing hope and even losing one's self.

In its more extreme condition, if depression sets in the result can cause tremendous damage. Therefore, use every trick you can think of to bring yourself, and those you manage, to a state of stability and balance.

For instance, you may need to disguise some unpleasant occurrence, pretending that it is a temporary situation. Or position it as one where acceptable solutions are possible. If it means putting on a happy face, do so. All these approaches will help immeasurably to relieve those individuals who may be disheartened and are looking for someone in whom they can unburden themselves.

Therefore, as you manage your people infuse them with the mantra, "Never give up hope." Get them to recognize that there are always possibilities and potential solutions worth considering. As for the competitive marketplace, there are numerous fight-back strategies and approaches for you to create opportunities – which are the central themes throughout this book.

Also, draw on case examples and past events where you and others overcame tough obstacles. From such an examination, you can take away valuable attitude-changing lessons, such as:

- If you believe you did damage, then believe you can repair.
- If you believe you made wrong choices, then believe you can find correct solutions.
- If you lost a competitive encounter, then believe you can win another day. Things can go from the very worst to the very best in just an instant.

Also, in the process of tuning-in, understand the differences between sadness and depression. Depression is really anger, perhaps a complaint against a spiritual entity for not giving you what you want. But when you are sad, your heart is repentant. As a parallel lesson, your ability to forget frees you from the burdens of the past.

> ***Key point:***
>
> Use every trick you can think of to bring yourself, and those you manage, to a state of stability and balance. Avoid depression at any cost.

6. *Seek an intuitive awakening*

Opportunities require a level of thought beyond your conscious level. That level translates to the remarkable value of intuition.

Think of intuition as an inner voice that presents you with possible courses of action. It unlocks the mind and guides you by means of flashes of insights, ideas, images, metaphors, or symbols. "The intuitive mind tells the rational thinking mind where to look next," declared the renowned Dr. Jonas Salk.

While intuition is often thought of as something elusive, spontaneous, and outside your control, nevertheless, it is possible to make intuition more accessible and more reliable. It begins by paying attention to your feelings. That means starting with a quiet mind and turning off the constant monologue that clutters the mind.

You then adopt a mindset where simply knowing transcends reason. Just perceiving possibilities is also an intuitive function. Of course, you can never be certain what the outcome of a decision is going to be. But you can have a strong intuitive sense of the direction you want to pursue.

Yet such a leap of understanding isn't in opposition to or a substitute for reason. And it certainly is not in conflict with the input of reliable market intelligence. Intuition is inner power that you use in addition to reason and factual information. In effect, there is an integration of intuition with the logical and linear thinking mind.

To make intuition work, you have to learn to hold attention on something for more than a few seconds, which can be a real challenge internally. For some, that also means emptying the mind of the emotional baggage that upsets, angers, and creates a chaotic state of mind. It means letting go and being non-judgmental.

Key point:

Intuition is inner power that you use in addition to reason and factual information.

You may have to personalize how you reach the receptive state where your intuition can flourish. It may be through meditation, solitude, being out in nature alone and quiet, or using slow breathing techniques.

The object is to quiet the feelings, quiet the body, quiet the mind, and be left with a kind of inner knowing. In the silence you learn the most about intuition. It is in this period of incubation that you let a problem just sit and you take time out.

Other approaches include using mental imagery, which is more associated with thinking and tends to be the type of intuition used by business executives, especially entrepreneurs, who tend to be highly intuitive.

In all methods, a common requirement is trusting yourself. Then you can trust your intuition. Keeping track of the accuracy of your intuitive decisions will give you an indication of whether your mind is prepped for intuition to thrive.

The benefits come when you can perceive possibilities in the future. In its most practical business application, intuition applies to developing a strategic business plan where the first planning step is to develop a mission (or vision) statement for your company or business unit, or to define a long-term strategic direction for a product line.

Anything that breaks new ground, provides a future-directed vision, or pushes you beyond the boundaries of what you already know, is intuitive. If any mystery exists about intuition, it is that people seem to get information and they don't know how they got it. Mathematicians, for example, can arrive at theorems that have never been proven before, just through their intuition.

"No problem is solved by the same consciousness that created it," observed the celebrated Albert Einstein who was known for his reliance on intuition.

What is required is a shift in consciousness, and through this shift you tap the subconscious mind to show you the way to solve a problem, which is revealed as intuition. What follows is for you to use logic, reason, and market research to follow-up on the intuition for proof and validation. However, if time does not permit that luxury and you must react to a severe competitive situation, then you have sound reason to trust in your intuition.

As for the creative moment, it is often an intuitive leap that enables you to see things you haven't noticed before. It could be a new perception, as if you acknowledge what you already knew, but may have forgotten. It is a sense of inner understanding, rather than something that you need to learn about. Again, being intuitive is trusting yourself.

We are all equipped with intuition. It is built in. It is pragmatic. It solves problems. It identifies opportunities that may not be seen with conscious vision. In the early stages of your intuitive journey, it may seem that the awakening is rejecting you and blocking your efforts. Yet, it is important for you and your employees to stay on course. Just don't give up.

In time, the barriers will disappear. Too often there is the faulty notion that everything has to go exactly your way, within your timeframe.

Yet, believe that none of the effort you labored over is wasted, even if you don't achieve what you are striving for immediately. Your work may just be a stepping stone to some larger outcome. Another side effect is that you will be stronger and better for the attempt, which may be essential to reach the next plateau of activity.

Further, do all you can to avoid being frustrated by the inevitable obstacles you will encounter. They exist by design to increase the intensity of your desire to reach your goal. The greater your goal, the greater the yearning you will need to achieve it.

Therefore, adopt this mindset: You are never given an obstacle you cannot overcome. That comment does suggest that you and your employees meet the obstacles half-way by means of dedicated training, on-going motivation, and effective planning.

Therefore, develop a working environment of positive anticipation, words of encouragement, and forward thinking. To the extent that you can, display matching behavior that strengthens the mind, calms the emotions, and leaves little room for despair.

Nevertheless, there is the dangerous and aggravating reality that despite your best efforts, despair, as if in a desolate deep hole, does irritate and feed depression. This negative emotion could result from the following:

- Misguided decisions in planning
- Violations of the fundamental rules of leadership
- Inability to align your strategy with the company's culture
- Lack of reliable competitive intelligence
- Inadequate knowledge about the rules of competitive strategy

In those circumstances, you have to put your own mind in a receptive state and listen intuitively for answers. Where appropriate, call out clearly for solutions. Ask: "What are the opportunities?" The sounds vibrate and send energy signals to the mind, which often sets-off intuitive inspiration.

Such understanding means that you know in the innermost parts of your mind that solutions do exist. Therefore, no matter how severe a competitive situation, success is not beyond salvaging and not beyond your reach. It is indeed within your grasp.

For instance, solutions could be in the psychological and physical areas. The ones worth considering and exploiting were always there. Somehow they got mixed-in with the errors. These areas are covered in the following chapters.

7. *Reach the hearts of those you manage*

Numerous psychologists, business scholars, consultants, and executives use the insightful and sensitive term, heart, to collectively describe the underlying emotional qualities by which a manager leads. For example, order or confusion, commitment or indifference, boldness or cowardice are emotions that typically dominate the heart.

When applied to a competitive market situation, it is essential for you to influence and, to the extent possible, control your rival's actions. The aim is to frustrate the competing manager and move against him.

That is, aggravate your competitor and confuse him into indecision or into making hasty and unwise choices. You thereby rob him of the heart to plan with the winning spirit and courage suitable to the demands of an embattled marketplace. Therefore, in your hands this psychological aspect of human nature becomes an effective strategy tool to unbalance a competitor and exploit an opportunity.

Heart also reflects in your behavior and ability to perform as an inspiring leader. In effect, your attitude filters down and impacts the performance of those members of your staff who might be robbed of spirit and deprived of courage.

Accordingly, managing requires, among other traits, for you to project confidence and display the discipline that will prevent you from caving in on every obstacle. Heart is how you create stability out of confusion, enthusiasm from discouragement, and bravery out of cowardice.

Therefore, actively reach out to win your employees' hearts. Encourage them. Convey confidence in their work and attitude. Offer appreciation, and wherever possible, provide tangible security through rewards as well as through meaningful training.

On the other hand, if you personally lose courage, a winning spirit, and decisiveness to identify opportunities, then your ability to lead under stressful situations is at serious risk.

Key point:

Actively reach out to win your employees' hearts. Encourage them. Convey confidence in their work and attitude.

What, then, is behind this managerial trait called *heart*?

Are the mannerisms inborn or learned? Some behaviors may be naturally innate. Or they can be deliberately instilled in early childhood.

Others may be shaped by deep-seated experiences, which leave individuals with permanent personality traits that are displayed throughout the early stages of life. Or they remain inactive until triggered later in life by a severe set of circumstances.

How, then, is this psychological dimension called heart applied to the hard-nosed, pragmatic work connected with creating opportunities? Let's examine the following key factors that encompass a business: vision, culture, strategy, planning, training and development, customer orientation, employing people, and technology.

- *Vision*

Develop a habit of looking forward in time for at least three to five years. Picture in your mind what you want your company or business unit to look like. Describe what business your company will be in. Indicate which markets you will likely serve. List the range of services your customers will likely require. Find out what types of technologies will probably be in use.

This effort is not crystal-ball gazing, but a defined process that permits you to take into account a variety of internal and external factors[3]. The process is also part of the procedure for developing a strategic business plan[4].

Notwithstanding the current economic, political, or terrorist events, it is still possible to determine a future direction. A well-defined vision, or strategic direction, keeps you focused and prevents wandering into badly chosen and strength-consuming situations. It improves your ability to make strategic choices in such diverse areas as market selection, product development, technology, global competition, or the Internet.

- *Culture*[5]

Take into account the history and values that define the culture of your organization and people. As you develop a vision of where you want your business to be in three to five years, also determine if the company's culture is in harmony with reaching your goals.

Even with a casual look at how your employees react in a variety of competitive situations, you should be able to determine if the behaviors and attitudes of individuals, from sales reps to senior managers, are equal to the task of performing efficiently in a changeable economy.

---

3. Internal and external factors are listed in Chapter 5.
4. Chapter 8 provides a detailed outline for a Strategic Business Plan. In particular, view the section on developing a Strategic Direction.
5. A company's culture is defined as the invisible web of values, things, ideas, and behavioral patterns that exist within the organization.

Will they be proactive or passive; confident or worried; daring or timid? Depending on what you observe, are there some company principles, a set of fundamental values, or a collection of built-in beliefs by which you can unite individuals and energize them to change a critical situation into a positive one?

Culture is significant because it is the soul of an organization. It defines the organization's identity. It highlights the principles for which it stands. Unfortunately, company culture is an often-overlooked factor when you need to arouse individuals into action and declare your leadership. Yet it is pivotal to the vitality and ultimately the successful outcome of any effort to create fresh opportunities.

In a different time period, General William T. Sherman observed, "There is a soul to an army as well as to the individual man. And no general can accomplish the full work of his army unless he commands the soul of his men, as well as their bodies and legs."

Sherman's insightful comment impacts directly on a business organization. It bears on all the previous discussions about your employees' mindset, attitudes, and outlook.

Key point:

Culture is the soul of an organization. It defines the organization's identity. Unfortunately, it is an often overlooked factor in motivating individuals into action.

- *Strategy*

Cultivate the vital skills to develop and implement strategies. Defined as actions to achieve your objectives, strategies include:

(a) estimating your competitive situation, (b) utilizing business intelligence, (c) developing a flexible and responsive organization, (d) locating your optimum market position, and (e) practicing the art of maneuver.

In effect, while a leader defines the strategy; strategy defines the caliber of the leader.[6] As such, you are virtually obligated to give serious attention to understanding the foundation elements of strategy: speed, indirect approach, concentration, alternative objectives, and unbalancing competition. (These five elements are covered in Chapter 3.)

Moreover, look to strategy as a natural extension of vision and culture. Meaning: A vision without a strategy remains a vague impression. A corporate culture without defined objectives and proactive strategies shrinks to an ill-defined, unwieldy collection of good intentions.

- *Planning*

Hone your planning skills. Central to your business success is a strategic business plan that reflects your vision for the enterprise. The planning process guides you to evaluate the past, view the future, assess competition, and examine internal and external conditions.

If the strategic business plan is handled correctly, the tangible outputs would provide you with a list of opportunities in such areas as differentiated products and value-added services to satisfy existing customers and newly identified prospects.

The plan is also one of the best mediums to connect all levels of personnel. Based on a need to know, it provides precise statements related to the strategic direction, objectives, and strategies of your organization or business unit. As a communications device, it has the far-reaching advantage of improving employee morale. (See Action step 1 in the beginning of this chapter.)

6. Strategy also can be defined to include a broader perspective: It is the art of coordinating the means (money, human resources, and materials) to achieve the end (profit, customer satisfaction, and company growth) as defined by company policy and objectives.

- *Training and Development*

Concentrate on continuous training of your personnel. In many marginal situations, trained personnel often turn the tide and decide the success or failure of a campaign - or even the total enterprise.

Training impacts directly on overall company performance and efficiency. Ultimately, it affects virtually every operation of the business.

For instance, maneuvers often require daring and roundabout moves to throw competitors off track. Such maneuvers can only take place by individuals who exhibit the skills and discipline honed through ongoing training.

Often, there are situations where competitors may surprise you with an innovative product or deep price cuts. Here, too, decisive strategies require trained individuals with the ability and confidence to correctly assess the situation and take positive action.

The unfaltering lessons endure: Only the skilled will survive. Conversely, the unskilled will disappointment.

As has been shown, the quality of your individuals is far superior to quantity. Consequently, don't sacrifice quality. If you do, there is failure — unless the competition is far inferior.

While no situation offers certain results, it is self-evident that the skilled and watchful eyes of well-trained individuals can turn a drawback to an advantage and prevent a disadvantage turning into a route.

Who, then, is ultimately responsible to assure a prompt and successful response to a competitive move? Plainly, the accountability for bottom-line results remains with you.

Training your personnel to act promptly and correctly so they don't falter is an essential factor in managerial competence. By inference, then, you create the environment where opportunities are developed. The subsequent action they take and how they perform are in your hands.

- *Customer Orientation*

Initiate a customer-oriented mindset among all those who surround you. In this era of global competition, it should be apparent that a total customer focus is mandatory for a firm's existence. Yet, it must be restated:

Your role is to establish a customer orientation as the operating philosophy behind what is generally accepted as a 21st Century market-driven organization. Expressed differently, a customer-driven orientation justifies a company's existence.

Over the past four decades, a customer orientation evolved as the centerpiece of modern business doctrine. In turn, it defines the broadened status of marketing in such an organization:

Marketing is a total system of interacting business activities designed to price, promote, and distribute want-satisfying products and services to consumers and business-to-business users in a competitive environment at a profit.

Clearly, the customer orientation, encompassing every activity of the organization, is embedded in that definition.

- *Employing People*

Look to your people, with all their habits, mannerisms, and subtleties, as a focal point of your leadership. People are the means by which you implement business strategy.

The following four areas cover a multitude of people issues:

First, employing people connects with maneuver. It means you don't sacrifice your human and financial resources through costly confrontations. For instance, should a competitor attempt to leave a market, do not intervene directly. Let the rival leave at its own time and pace. Allow it an easy way out without imposing any exit barriers. Where possible even go so far as to help eliminate barriers.

Second, don't lead your people blindly into seemingly profitable areas left open by an exiting competitor without first assessing if there are unseen traps, such as an inefficient supply chain, disgruntled customers, or changing technologies for which you are not prepared. Find out the exact reasons for the competitor giving up a market.

Third, communicate fully and completely with your staff. That is, be with them physically and emotionally. Respond to them face-to-face, wherever possible. Use tangible signs of support, beyond the well-intended personalized memos. Most often, they will only respond to what they see. Various mottoes used by leaders illustrate the maxim, such as "Remain visible." "Manage by walking around." "Don't expect what you don't inspect."

Fourth, pay strict attention to the highly sensitive issue of how you pair-up people or form a team. Try to position your best individuals with your weakest performers. Join them, so that one supports the other and the guidelines of performance are clearly observed. Doing so offers a unity of effort that can be monitored.

Thus, aggressive individuals do not operate out of phase with the weaker performers. Also, a coordinated team effort is more likely to achieve maximum results without an independent Rambo-style action. Consequently, holding the aggressive ones in line is as important as forcing the timid to act.

These guidelines will assist in using your people to the best advantage in developing fresh opportunities.

- *Technology*

Embrace technology. The prime differentiator, now and likely for the future, is how you grasp the immense possibilities of technology. More than ever, technology will continue to have far-reaching effects on R&D, manufacturing productivity, marketing, distribution, and customer service.

In particular, the current Internet age presents vastly different situations from what existed during the previous decades. For instance, as a 21st Century manager you now face an increasing number of global competitors. Internet entrepreneurs leap into so-called secure markets and whisk away once loyal customers.

Mind-boggling new technology harnesses innovative products customized for customers' exacting specifications. And new forms of communication connect sellers to waiting customers with amazing speed in an ever-spreading global arena.

Developing a Positive Mindset and Attitude

For the most part, your employees' psychological frame of mind outweighs their physical surroundings. While the physical location, furniture, and similar trappings are important, they can never be as vital as the spirit and the enthusiasm of your employees.

For instance, during the early stages of a campaign spirits are sharp, excitement is high. During the middle stages enthusiasm tends to decline; focus is often diverted to other real or invented events. In the later stages of the cycle, thoughts often turn to trivial issues or wishful desires. Accordingly, when maneuvering for competitive opportunity, watch the morale of your staff.

In practice, therefore, carefully observe a market campaign in action. Their attention should be keen and enthusiastic. Stay alert and intervene only when attention is diverted, spirits downcast, morale marred, or you see obvious mistakes develop.

Recognize, too, that attitude-adjusting and morale-building are essential parts of your duties. Enhance these parts through training, appreciation, recognition, security, and all the guidelines provided in this chapter. In the end, your aim is toward active participation and mutual commitment to goals and objectives.

As for you, remain calm and firm. Try not to be easily unbalanced by negative events. In that condition of physical and mental composure, you are in a better state of mind to reduce any emotions of anger, fear, worry, or resentment. If left unattended, those feelings can cause you to lose grip of the situation and possibly end up losing your advantage to a competitor.

Consequently, responsibilities for the emotional and spirited well-being of your employees, as well as yourself, are in your hands:

You trigger the emotions and set the tone for performance. You develop enthusiasm which generates excitement. You show confidence which spawns self-assurance in others.

There is always hope! Mastering the prescribed guidelines in this chapter and those that follow will result in building your inner strength. You will gain the confidence and resilience to project definite objectives through which to guide decisions and implement new opportunities.

3

Project Optimistic Leadership

"I can't define leadership, but whatever it is, I've got it."

General George C. Patton, Jr.

Even with such an inconclusive statement by a world-renowned leader, there is enough evidence to suggest that leadership and managerial performance do contain natural as well as learned skills. And if the acquired skills merge with an individual's innate abilities, the outstanding leader is clearly distinguished from the mediocre manager.

Thus, we come down to the mental or psychological dimensions of leadership. Numerous authors, academics, consultants, and other practitioners lay claim to understanding and teaching the components of leadership. What follows is a summary of the generally accepted leadership qualities and, if adapted, can enhance your ability to manage people, resources, and implement effective business-building opportunities.

The primary qualities include: insightfulness, straightforwardness, compassion, boldness, and strictness.

If *insightful*, you recognize early-on the impact of new competitors coming into your market space. Or you spot changes in your customers' buying behavior, shifts in your industry's use of new technologies, and environmental trends, such as the "green" movement on your business.

If *straightforward*, your employees have no doubt how and when rewards or reprimands would be handed out.

If *compassionate*, you respect your employees, appreciate their hard work, and empathize with them during stressful times.

If *bold*, you find innovative ways to market your company or product by seizing opportunities; and you avoid getting bogged down in indecision.

If *strict*, you are dedicated to the long-term objectives of your company. In turn, your people respect your discipline and optimistic outlook.

Now, let's apply those positive leadership qualities to the realities of creating opportunities in a challenging competitive environment:

First, marketplace encounters mean that you have to work with the best information available.

Second, it means acting boldly and implementing strategies with speed — even where data about your competitor is sketchy, and despite uncertainties.

Third, you should rely on inner-support from intuitive guidance when you feel weighed down with apprehension. That is, drawing on your ability to boost your courage and determination by following your instincts, however faint, to find the proper path.[1]

Some managers realize they must be strong-minded; at the same time they sense the dangers of a flawed decision. They are not sure of what is before them. Even if in the habit of acting with speed, the more they linger with the dangers of indecision, the more doubtful they become.

One reliable approach to reduce the level of anxiety is to make estimates beforehand. Therefore, use every bit of available market intelligence you can get hold of. Then develop alternative courses of action. Doing so, prepares you to take clear-thinking action at

1. See discussion on the high value of intuition further on in this chapter and in Chapter 2.

a given moment and thereby alleviate the unsettling feeling that comes with indecisiveness.

> ***Key point:***
>
> Use every bit of available market intelligence available. Then develop alternative courses of action.

As for boldness it becomes a character trait only if it develops into a mental habit. It consists of actions grounded in steadfast determination and applied to a specific situation. There a number of brilliant managers who simply do not have what it takes to make timely and appropriate decisions. Often, this lack of courage is triggered by their innate fear of failure.

Therefore, it is in your best interest to arouse the inner feeling of courage. Then act. Doing so means facing the critical moments by pushing aside the negative feelings that creep into your mind and taking control of your actions.

Overcoming those sensations relies on training, discipline, and experience. Keep in mind that you are in a contest of mind against mind; your mind pitted against the mind of a competing manager who may be challenged by similar emotions. You want to be the one who prevails and moves forward. (See Table 3.1.)

Consider the extraordinary success of **Google Inc**. Much has been written about the bold and entrepreneurial approaches that founders Larry Page and Sergey Brin exhibited when they started operations in 2000. Even then, they showed their courage by going contrary to the sage advice of seasoned consultants and analysts who considered selling out for a mere pittance during those early days.

Industry watchers saw the behavioral patterns surface once again as the search giant quietly acquired a mobile-phone software company and began making forays into instant messaging, Wi-Fi Internet, and telephony businesses.

Where, then, did boldness play a role?

First, to maintain leadership in its existing business, Google had to keep innovating as the likes of Microsoft and Yahoo! actively searched for competing market positions.

Next, it took guts to enter new markets that were well protected by such giants as eBay, Motorola, Nokia, SBC Communications, and Verizon. Initially, Google had to play catch-up in those fields just to get a foothold. Then, they had to find ways to carve out new or unserved market niches, or enhance their position with unique applications of technology.

Table 3.1. Guidelines for Successful Leadership

- Hold fast to the definitive object of all business, which according to the late management scholar, Peter Drucker, is to "create a customer."
- Remove obstacles that deprive people from gaining pride in providing quality of service and in delivering innovative products.
- Break down inhibiting barriers within the company by establishing cross-functional teams of workers.
- Introduce a work environment where the emphasis is on junior managers leading, not merely supervising.
- Commit to long-term goals, such as developing leading-edge products or maintaining superior service and product quality.
- Eliminate the use of fear as a motivator.
- Encourage employees to express ideas; listen to them and respond.
- Promote self-improvement as an ongoing obligation.
- Institute continuing employee training and education to advance their skills, personal growth, and chances for career advancement.

BARRIERS TO EFFECTIVE LEADERSHIP

The following list identifies a variety of barriers that could hamper your ability to accomplish your goals; or in keeping with the theme of this book, create opportunities:

1. *Lack of trust by managers in their employees' discipline, capabilities, or skills.*

This factor is most serious. The best laid plans, your most ambitious goals, and the most vibrant business strategies are not going to work with inexperienced employees who lack the essential business skills.

Also, if they do not display a steadfast discipline or if they cannot demonstrate an aptitude for the job, your firm could be in trouble.

Consequently, if you show a lack of trust in some personnel, don't blame them entirely. It is your responsibility to maintain an environment where knowledge, ongoing training, and discipline stand out as the bedrock components of successful performance.

Understand, too, that a certain amount of attrition is desirable to maintain the agility, motivation, and energy to solve problems and identify moneymaking opportunities.

> ***Key point:***
>
> Maintain an environment where knowledge, ongoing training, and discipline stand out as the bedrock components of successful performance.

2. *Lack of trust by employees in their manager's ability to make correct decisions.*

This is a particularly troublesome problem should your staff's morale deteriorate and they lose confidence in your ability to deal with what they perceive as a hopeless situation that could threaten their jobs - and even the company. Here, again, skill, courage, and determination are necessary traits that require continuous reinforcement.

3. *Inadequate support from the owner or senior executives.*

If gaps in communication exist among various levels, the result is inadequate command and control. In turn, such a vacuum prevents timely support in such areas as: approving investments, shifting resources to secure a competitive position, or improving customer services.

Then, there is needed support for such essential projects as technology upgrades, new product development, and distribution. Beyond those areas is the back-up you need to pull together all the projects and activities and align them with your business plan.

4. *Disagreement and open confrontation with others about objectives, priorities, and strategies.*

Where individuals of equal rank cannot resolve difficulties independently, as a leader it is up to you to intervene. Where there are limited resources and numerous "great" proposals, it is typical and understandable that there will be disagreements, and even inner-fighting. That means resources must be allocated among many business proposals, all of which are vying for attention.

Inevitably, some plans get short-changed or receive an outright turndown. And even the winners suffer the effects of lost time that slows their efforts. Painfully, the lapse in time may give the edge to an alert competitor.

5. *Highly conservative and plodding company culture places a drag on getting projects moving.*

This is a tough barrier. Yet it is one that you must face. If your company's culture is out of synch with the competitive environment, and if you are not in position to change the culture, you must adapt plans to the existing culture with the aim of moving as rapidly as possible.

6. *Lack of urgency in developing new products to deal with short product life cycles.*

It is no secret that products exist in a short timeframe and in a commercial world that clamors for faster/cheaper/smaller. Where that basic knowledge is not fully internalized by you and others, or acted upon quickly, results can be shattering.

The life cycle issue has gained so much importance that software developers such as **USG, SAP**, and **Dassault Systems** sell product life-cycle management (PLM) software. It is the fastest-growing segment of the corporate software market, growing 14% faster than any other segment.

PLM software allows people to coordinate their work within a specified stage of the product life cycle, regardless of location. Individuals post ideas for new products. Engineers work on designing 3D prototypes. Manufacturers lay out production schedules. With virtually no limitations, scores of people can participate on a single project from anywhere there's a Web connection.

7. *No simplified system of control exists, so that cumbersome committees prolong deliberation that results in unwarranted delays.*

In a small organization the owner or president is at the helm. He or she is in a unique position to control planning and execution. Thus, decisions are less likely to be misinterpreted, delayed, or contested. Plans can be implemented with consistency and speed.

However, should roadblocks exist that prevent decisions being made in a timely manner, an unwieldy process exists that can result in the following drawbacks:

- Loss of time recovering market information.
- Loss of time sending orders forward to key individuals and staff.
- Lack of full knowledge of the situation by the owner or president.
- Reduction of key individuals' involvement in issues that affect the availability of resources.

Therefore, a more flexible, smaller organization can potentially achieve greater market penetration because it has the capacity to adjust to varying circumstances more rapidly. It can thereby concentrate at the decisive point before a larger competitor has a chance to respond.

Key point:

A smaller organization can concentrate at the decisive point before a larger competitor has a chance to respond.

8. *Threats from aggressive competitors strike fear among your employees, which damages morale and results in lost momentum.*

Psychological impressions can create perceptions of success or failure in an individual's mind, as if they were actual physical encounters with competitors. Thus, perception, what the mind can conjure up, believe, and then react to, is indeed reality.

Such perceptions feed employees' reactions, which generate a set of emotions. Some are correct, others distorted. That means employees will react to signs they choose to interpret and believe through observation, feel, or from the inevitable rumors — right or wrong.

What follows is that your employees' morale could falter based on the slightest signs of what they perceive as a reversal. Such warnings could include: failed performance of a new product, reduced profits, changing customer behavior, or competitors grabbing your key customers.

Then, there are the sudden changes in the company, such as the resignation of a key employee or the shrinking of operations that can send shivers through the employee ranks.

It is *discipline, training, leadership, ambition, company culture,* and *self-confidence* that will greatly influence how employees will react to these signs.

Let's look more closely at each influence:

- *Discipline*

As pointed above and in Chapter 2, toughening-up employees to withstand the natural swings that exist in a hard-hitting competitive market takes a good deal of leadership skill. It entails a great deal of sensitivity on your part, if you have any intention of altering their attitudes and behaviors. This is particularly essential when the natural inclination is to retreat from the realities of an uncertain and erratic economy.

Therefore, your aim is to inspire individuals to make courageous save-my-company, save-my-job efforts and turn potential defeat into victory.

Accordingly, maintain a compassionate awareness of what the psychological effects can have on your business strategies – as well as on your ability to manage your subordinates.

For instance, if individuals are placed in a no-escape predicament and if faced with the bleak outcome of dismissal, they are not likely to back away from self-interest. Instead, they will often use their utmost creativity and energy to fight out of the tight spot.

Thus, a real or perceived threat often creates remarkable behavior among individuals – if inspired by an energetic manager with a disciplined strategy for survival, followed by a plan for a burst of growth.

For example, one small company that markets organic fertilizer and similar environment-friendly products reported a grass-roots change in behavior among its employees. When informed of tough market conditions by the president with little funds for marketing, individuals on their own initiative became their own marketing force.

They went on the road and visited retailers to check on displays, talked-up their products, and chatted with customers. Instead of taking a plane, staying in a hotel, and charging meals, several persons drove their cars more than 1,000 miles each, going so far as to sleep in their back seats.

- *Training*

There is the pragmatic truth that if employees are unaccustomed to the rigors of travel and long hours of work, they will worry and hesitate at the moment when levelheaded decisions are needed to handle severe competitive conditions. It is here that meaningful training pays for itself.

What exactly do you want the training to accomplish? Use the following guidelines and modify them for your particular use.

First and foremost, within the framework of this book and the nature of a competitive global economy, assume that a competitor will vigorously confront your aggressive moves to create opportunities. Therefore, aim your training so that you create a state of readiness to meet an opponent going after your company and your market. The key word is readiness.

Take these steps:

- Set up interactive communications within your organization that encourages innovation and shows individuals how to harness maximum energy among all levels of personnel. Do so by using the power of positive words, optimistic attitudes, forward looking plans, full participation with a customer-driven outlook, and all the guidelines suggested in Chapter 1 and this one.
- Teach individuals how to develop a business plan, so that the mission (or vision) for the organization is internalized by individuals, objectives are written to complement the mission statement, strategies are pinpointed to achieve the objectives, and products and services are identified to drive the organization forward.
- Train your people in the vital importance of maintaining ongoing competitive intelligence (CI). This is the key component to developing and implementing competitive strategies.

  Here's the central idea behind CI: If you know your rival's plans, you are able to monitor his moves. Then you can figure on which strategies will likely succeed and those to avoid.

Also, you can probe the competitor's market position, expose strengths and weaknesses, and know where you will likely face tough opposition. You then have lead-time to take appropriate actions.

Taken as a whole, you enjoy the advantage of knowing where your competitor's strengths are formidable and where weak. What better way is there for you to establish credibility and motivate your staff to deal with potentially harmful situations?

- Initiate training that gives your group a fighting edge. As part of that training, set up a cross-functional team to gain maximum input and create a high-level of buy-in from various points of view. (See Table 3.3, Functions and Responsibilities of a Cross-Functional Team.)

Such training aims toward innovation. As applied to readiness, it focuses on truly imaginative and differentiated products or processes, and not just cosmetic embellishments of what already exists. This type of training may require a new level of thought consistent with a Web-based economy. In particular, it requires a company culture that encourages innovation as a prerequisite for readiness.

However, the reality is that you and your company may not have the resources and other capabilities to come up with dazzling new-age products. Instead, your innovation may come from providing fresh marketing approaches, after-sales services, new packaging ideas, financing plans, or providing warehousing and distributing systems for other companies.

As for formal training, many small businesses are turning to Web-based job training modules. These can be much less expensive than in-house training, cover a range of pertinent job topics and can be completed on your employees' schedules. In many cases vendors can provide training modules that are customized to your company's needs.

Overall, training aims to create an environment of trust and understanding, whereby subordinates are encouraged to seize the initiative and act with a sense of purpose and loyalty. For employees, it is no giant leap between thinking their leader is disloyal to the organization, to thinking their leader will be disloyal to them as well.

Key point:

Aim your training so that you create a state of readiness to meet an opponent and target an opportunity.

- *Ambition*

One of the essential qualities of a leader is ambition. There never was an outstanding leader without ambition. It is the mainspring of all actions. But for pragmatic meaning, ambition must be worthy of the organization's mission and not a pathway to solitary power.

Ambition is difficult to separate from courage. In analyzing great leaders it is generally impossible to decide which of their actions in the face of severe problems bore the mark of boldness or that of ambition. Both are characteristics of the truly outstanding leader.

It is constructive ambition and the intense desire to excel that stimulates ambition in others. The magic of winning always arouses determination, which gives momentum to the organization. Therefore, nurturing positive ambition is another prime duty of the leader.

Yet the unwelcome reality exists that unrestrained personal ambition does live on, with all its excesses and potentially harmful outcomes. It is uncontrolled raw ambition that destroys employees' careers and the economic livelihoods of communities in which the organizations operate. Such excesses and scandalous executive behavior that decimated even the loftiest organizations first came to light during the recession period of 2008–09.

Consequently, if you seek competence in leadership, understand how the power of corporate culture interfaces with ambition. Culture is the cement that binds together all the qualities and gives an organization a unique personality and forms the underpinnings of unity.

> ***Key point:***
>
> Winning arouses ambition, which gives momentum to the organization. Therefore, nurturing positive ambition is another prime duty of the leader.

- *Communications*

What you should strive for is clear, organized communication that conveys information about the following: long- and short-term objectives, strengthening customer relationships, trends about the market and industry, and intelligence about competitors. Then there are the tactical details that influence advertising, selling, and customer service.

Clear communication also relates to an uncluttered organization system that permits the easy flow of information up and down the organization. (For additional information see, pt. 7 of Barriers to Effective Leadership.)

- *Culture*

The company's culture, made up of its history, values, and behaviors, shapes the attitudes and relationships you have with customers and suppliers. For instance, an outlook that leans on an overconfident attitude of "we've got the market locked up" often translates to complacency and ends with defeat.

Such feelings tend to dry up creativity and stifle the inner drive to push for excellence. It draws-off the adrenalin that comes from fighting within a performance-based marketplace.

The marketplace is littered with one-time leaders in such fields as automobiles, electronics, metals, and consumer goods. Some companies in those industries turned around the last moment; others were acquired or just went bankrupt.

The mindset was usually supported by the inaccurate notion that high market share means security, which was often followed by a passive defense of that market position. Those conditions at one time or another faced such high-profile companies as **Xerox, EMC,** and **Hewlett-Packard**. All, however, have aggressively pulled out of the slump.

Start-ups, as well as those companies still in the beginning stages of growth, are also beginning to focus on the importance of aligning their corporate culture with growth strategies.

For instance, **Twitter Inc**. co-founders Biz Stone and Evan Williams looked to grow beyond the phenomenal introduction of their micro-blogging service. As part of their strategy, they emphasized growing Twitter slowly in order to find people who fit with its culture. The culture for Stone and Williams is partially defined through a variety of rituals, such as family-style lunches and weekly "teas," or happy hours.

Key point:

Train personnel to acquire a way of thinking and a culture that is totally customer-driven.

You can achieve excellence as a leader when your people are disciplined and committed to the organization's cultural values. Excellence in leadership, however, does not mean perfection. On the contrary, an excellent leader allows subordinates room to learn from their mistakes as well as from their successes.

In such a positive climate, people work to improve and take the risks necessary to learn. A leader who sets a standard of "zero defects, no mistakes" is also saying "Don't' take any chances. Don't try anything you can't already do perfectly, and don't try anything new."

- *Self-confidence*

Embedded in excellent leadership is the enormous power of self-confidence that you will perform correctly in a critical situation. Self-confidence comes from the inner-feelings that you are competent in your job.

And what do your employees absolutely desire? They want a self-confident leader who can accurately assess conditions, knows what needs to be done, and demonstrates a capability to take appropriate actions. A self-confident mind is not just capable of strong mental exertions. It is one that in the midst of tackling severe problems can maintain its equilibrium regardless of internal turmoil.

What about your self-confidence?

To expect that you will remain calm and reserved in every situation is asking for a superhuman effort. The agonizing feeling of failure is not a fabrication or an illusion. It is a conscious realization, for instance, that a competitor may be superior for reasons previously unforeseen and may be preventing you from taking advantage of an opportunity.

Such conditions could legitimately cause a sudden collapse of all your hopes, a breaking down of self-confidence. Instead of working energetically with subordinates to stem the tide, each person fears that his efforts will be useless, hesitates where he should move, and leaves everything to fate.

The essential point: Competitive encounters assume that human weaknesses do exist. These materialize as momentary negative impressions of events that can distract you from your overall objectives. You should put such disruptions into correct perspective immediately, however uncomfortable they may appear.

For instance, when you personally go into a local marketplace be watchful that you don't become sidetracked by an isolated incident. Instead, look at the event and fit it into the framework of the entire market scene. Then test it against the broader business objectives of your business plan.

Should your self-confidence begin to falter and you feel your problems weighing on you more heavily, take whatever steps you can to strengthen your determination, rekindle enthusiasm, and most importantly, instill renewed hope among all those you manage.

Do so by focusing on the business plan as a whole. Once again, it is vitally important that you retain a broad view of the whole situation. Understand, too, effective leadership strengthened by well thought out strategies can work as a counterbalance to temporary emotions. This will help you remain committed to implementing the business plan.

Also, when tempted to doubt the correctness of your decisions, keep your faith in the time-tested leadership qualities and strategy principles that follow in the rest of the chapters.

Key point:

Success is a matter of morale and your ability to engage heart, mind, and spirit.

MORALE: THE ENERGIZER

A vital responsibility of a leader is to heighten employee morale. This will energize you and your staff with the resolve to act decisively under competitive pressures.

Morale provides unity and taps the inner strengths of individuals. Most important, it prevents them from faltering when the stress increases due to harsh market conditions.

Then there is another reality: Some cavalier owners and managers never seem to worry about morale. No obstacles seem to bother them. "Here's what I want you to do. Now do it!" is a familiar command.

Most often, however, they experience incredible disorder in the follow-on moves. They are the great leaders for a day, until the moment when some negative outcome overwhelms them. The greater and more reliable reality is that achieving high-morale takes ongoing training, excellent leadership, and intimate concern for your employees' well-being.

In pragmatic terms, marketplace conflicts are generally in the hands of each individual. And never has individual initiative, triggered by the potent force of morale, had greater importance. This is especially so with the many daily incidents that go unseen, especially when you are drawn to the more visible competitive conditions that grab your attention.

What follows are wide-ranging guidelines that encompass morale.

> ***Key point:***
>
> High-morale takes ongoing training, excellent leadership, and intimate concern for your employees' well-being.

Morale Meets Technology

Potential problems arise where employee morale confronts technology. So much has been said about latching on to the wonders of technology, even if it means suppressing the human element.

Where such a conflict exists, nothing is likely to be more fatal to the organization. Meaning: The individual is still the most significant element in conducting business. More precisely, the dominant issue is that people must harmonize with technology to achieve any favorable opportunity.

Further, new technologies are almost valueless in the hands of dispirited employees, no matter what their number. It is therefore essential to work at developing their morale, which is often grounded to the organization's embedded culture.

Thus, cutting-edge technology and outstanding business strategies, even supported with superior resources, will languish if employees are not personally moved by morale and the driving will to succeed.

Morale Connects with the Power of Unity

Don't let individuals fend for themselves. In absolute terms, that means they must know that support exists at the head office – and from you. Also, they must see and feel your physical presence to absorb the psychological comfort and confidence that would sustain their morale and motivate them to keep trying, especially under adverse conditions. (See Chapter 2, Herzberg's factors affecting motivation.)

As for the power of unity, it is not the "Rambo" effect of individual actions that make high-performing employees. It is the collective efforts of individuals within teams interacting among themselves that cultivates unity. It is for you to encourage such interaction. Once again, this is the fundamental purpose of teams.

In the end, it is up to you to know your people best and understand the reasons behind highly-charged displays of behavior such as anguish and fear – or at the other extreme, courage and dogged determination.

Therefore, you can't be a stranger to your employees; it is your personal influence and nearness that affects morale. If they feel themselves no longer supported, it creates an uncertain situation for you.

Unity requires that you sustain confidence in your ability to lead. If, on the other hand, you are habitually gripped by fear, then you should give second thoughts about leading your group.

Unity is also nurtured by a cohesive corporate culture, which is reinforced by an ethical climate built on core values. A healthy culture fortifies your leadership role and helps guide your organization or business unit.

Consequently, depending on your position in the firm, seek to shape your company's or department's culture to support its vision, articulate the goals, and improve the overall performance through high morale.

The renowned former General Electric CEO Jack Welch expressed these points uniquely in his *Business Week* column:

"Enthusiasm never hurts, but real passion is sparked by people knowing why the organization is taking a certain path and what the journey will mean to them." (See Table 3.2, Morale and Its Impact on Creating Opportunities.)

> ***Key point:***
>
> You can't be a stranger to your employees; it is your influence and physical presence that affects morale.

Table 3.2. Morale and Its Impact on Creating Opportunities

- Morale fades when there is no inspiring goal to fight for.
- Morale weakens when employees work in a state of uncertainty.
- Poor communications affect morale with a corresponding serious effect on implementing strategies.
- Lack of commitment to a competitive strategy with a determination to win affects morale.
- Unethical behavior impacts morale.
- An inability to create a long-term vision and develop attainable objectives influences morale.
- Undisciplined behavior that readily gives in to fear affects morale.
- A leader who procrastinates and visibly displays an inability to handle responsibility affects morale.
- A leader who stifles employees' input has a negative influence on morale.
- A leader's inability to accurately assess a competitive situation affects morale.
- A leader, who does not know how to reach the heart, mind, and spirit of a group, instead shows more interest in his personal agenda, impacts morale.
- Morale suffers and defeats become competitive disasters without sufficient training of personnel.

Morale Aligns with Innovation

Innovation is the new differentiator. Therefore, use all your efforts to keep jobs stimulating. And should something significant result from employees' creativity, express appreciation publicly for jobs well done. Your approach is to be even-handed, open-minded, and fair-minded.

Further, in all initiatives associated with innovation, support your people, communicate a vision of growth, provide them with the resources to do their jobs, and motivate them to learn and grow. As important, stand by them if something goes awry. Or else you shut them down – along with creativity.

What follows is for you to establish criteria for evaluating innovation. You need to let the staff know how they will be measured. The frequently used measures for innovation include the following:

- Overall revenue growth attributed to innovations
- Percentage of total sales from new products or services
- Level of customer satisfaction
- Improvements in market share
- Comparisons of innovations measured against chief competitors by product category and market segment
- Actual number of new products or services launched
- Ratio of new product successes
- Other criteria required by your company

Morale Links with Trust

Trust supports morale. So, too, are your supportive words of encouragement, as well as the image you project of reliability, integrity, and competence. Make certain that such expressions are group-serving, and not self-serving.

Festering below trust, however, is the potentially explosive behavior of individuals, which is due to the impulsive nature of people. They nervously shrink back and find danger where they don't see any possibility of success.

Personnel also tend not to act as obedient robots; rather, they pose as anxious and restless individuals who wish to finish things quickly and know in advance where they are going.

The purpose of focusing on trust, therefore, is to overcome those negative feelings among individuals who, for a variety of life's experiences, mistrust and doubt. Some have valid reasons having been misinformed, mistrusted, and misled in the past. Nonetheless, it is your challenge to create trust and convince them that you have their best interests at heart.

Morale Sustains Momentum

When embroiled in a difficult situation, try to maintain momentum and keep the probability of success on your side. At times a problem may seem insurmountable. Nonetheless, you must act against this probability even when the likelihood of success is against you. Don't think of your undertaking as unreasonable or impossible. It is always reasonable and there are always possibilities.

Often, the determining factor for climbing out of a tough predicament and regaining the initiative is to lean heavily on the quality of your personnel. This is possible, however, where (1) you address key issues affecting their morale (see Table 3.2), (2) take initiatives to provide for their growth, and (3) create a feeling of unity within the group.

These three areas have as their underpinnings – spirited leadership, a clearly understood vision or objective, and competent business strategies. These attributes makes individuals carry on in spite of any inclination to concede defeat.

ACTION STEPS TO BUILD MORALE

The following list provides concrete approaches to build morale:

Set Ethical Standards

Built on honesty, integrity, and moral behavior. Encourage individuals to speak out against underhanded practices. To give authority to such standards, tie compensation not only to higher performance but also to higher ethical standards.

Encourage Constructive Communications

Included here is the somewhat common practice where individuals hoard vital information, especially technical data, and deny its access by others. The aim is to protect a job and create a power base. Here, too, bind individuals' compensation to compliance.

Reward Managers for Meaningful Performance

Promotion and increases in compensation are rewards for boosting productivity and focusing on innovation. Promotion also includes driving growth by developing new revenue streams.

Use a Team Approach

The emphasis is on building teams with responsibilities, such as searching for new vertical markets by devising strategies to reach emerging, neglected, or poorly served segments.

Support the Free Flow of Ideas

A foundation requirement to activate morale is communicating effectively up, down, and across levels. Doing so puts problems and opportunities out in the open and spurs the free flow of ideas to solve problems. Open communications also works to expose opportunities, encourages others to think creatively – and brings to light any damaging issues that would hamper a team's progress.

Encourage Questions

Welcome questions and use them. If you avoid questions, you create a damaging vacuum by preventing new opportunities from surfacing and stifling those individuals who would be motivated to act. Questions often trigger the creative process, as they open minds to explore areas not otherwise considered.

Delegate

Morale will rise if you challenge individuals and give them responsibility. Often they will surprise you with solutions to problems that may have eluded you. Delegating also sends a strong message of confidence that you can let go and permit creativity and initiative to take over.

Anticipate

Create an environment of expectation and excitement. It should also be your intention to set up the psychological environment that eagerly anticipates success. (Review Chapter 2.)

Prioritize

With input of others, prioritize and rank those opportunities worth exploiting and problems needing solutions. Not only do you maximize resources, you involve the team in viewing the big picture and understanding the reasons behind the prioritizing.

Set High Standards

Benchmark your activities and goals against the "best", regardless of company size. Also look beyond your field by examining other industries for ideas. You thereby inspire your people about what can be accomplished. In the process, try to draw meaningful parallels and allow their competitive spirits to flourish.

Show Genuine Interest

Be available. Listen to employees' problems, complaints, and other issues. Fundamental to building morale is demonstrating to your people that you are genuinely interested in them and their growth. That means being sincere and treating them as valued employees who have insight, experience, and special knowledge.

Respect Differences

Accept the viewpoint that others may not see things as you do. Therefore, recognize differences of opinion, especially where there are diverse backgrounds. This is particularly so where more and more interactions take place with individuals in offshore locations.

Be Candid

Within the range of what is permissible or confidential, explain your actions to your employees. Provide information and guidance on matters that affect their security. (Review Herzberg's concepts cited in Chapter 2.) Keep your people up-to-date on all business matters affecting them. Also tackle unfounded rumors before they do damage.

Stay Positive

Avoid displaying anxiety or worry. During times of intense pressure, sidestep disclosing your concerns or fears to your personnel. Instead, present a problem as a challenge that can be turned to an opportunity through a unified team effort.

Monitor Performance

The object here is to tackle problems and correct situations before they fester. This process is also the basis for further training and creating a productive agenda for group meetings.

> ***Key point:***
>
> Avoid displaying anxiety or worry. During times of intense pressure, sidestep disclosing your concerns or fears to your personnel.

BARRIERS TO BUILDING MORALE

Undoubtedly and realistically, barriers to building morale will appear. The most significant ones are the following:

Lack of Planning Skills

Planning within a team setting is a unifying activity. Therefore, it is in your best interest to hone those skills that foster a collaborative approach. There are numerous formats for developing plans. Most have similar characteristics. Follow any of the popular formats, or use a standardized one that already exists in your firm. (See a format for a Strategic Business Plan in Chapter 8.)

Yet, within the context of building morale and unity, just acquiring planning skills is not enough. Rather, the more relevant issue is your team's ability to *think strategically*. That means honing skills that permit you and others to look forward in to the future while maintaining a down-to-earth need to initiate short-term actions. (See Table 3.3, Functions and Responsibilities of a Cross-Functional Team.)

> ***Key point:***
>
> Strengthening planning skills opens the mind to abundant possibilities.

Table 3.3. Functions and Responsibilities of a Cross-Functional Team

Functions include:

- Defining the direction of the business or product line. This is also known as a vision or mission statement.
- Analyzing the environmental, industry, customer, and competitive situations.
- Developing short- and long-term objectives and strategies.
- Preparing product, market, supply chain, and quality plans to implement competitive strategies.

Responsibilities include:

- Creating and recommending new or additional products and services.
- Approving all alterations or modifications of a major nature.
- Acting as a formal communications channel from the market back to internal departments.
- Planning and implementing strategies throughout the product life cycle.
- Developing programs to improve market position and profitability.
- Identifying market or product opportunities in light of changing consumer buying patterns.
- Coordinating efforts with various functions to achieve short- and long-term objectives.
- Organizing efforts for exchanging new market or product opportunities among groups or individuals.
- Developing a strategic business plan.

Lack of Resourcefulness and Drive

This barrier translates into being short of imagination, innovation, and all those factors that are generally understood to mean creativity. Herein is the crux of any firm's problems and consequently its opportunities; namely, to create innovative products, outfight and outperform competitors, and win firm footings in growth markets.

Lack of Vision

This barrier to morale can be addressed for the most part by getting individuals actively involved in developing strategic business plans. Here, again, standard formats exist. Most of them begin by developing a mission statement or strategic direction, which means creating a vision for your firm, business unit, or product line.

Lack of Self-development

One of the identifiable characteristics of a well-run organization is a system for ongoing learning, which leads to greater proficiency on-the-job and to career advancement. Self-development is certainly part of the morale factor and includes all the ingredients that go into your company's value system.

Lack of Self-confidence

This morale barrier shows up in a manager's indecisiveness, lack of vision, unwillingness to attack a problem, or reluctance to pursue an opportunity with vigor and boldness. Such displays of negative behavior and leadership are apparent to the employees.

Like an epidemic, these damaging traits can spread to all those who are exposed to them. If the lack of self-confidence cannot be converted to a positive attitude through self-motivation or with outside assistance, then the manager should step down before any further harm is done. In such an instance, another manager should take over day-to-day operations.

Procrastination

This barrier is the enemy of speed and is the sure way to dampen morale. Fast-changing consumer demands, global outsourcing, open-source software, near instant movement of capital across oceans, electronic transfers of knowledge, and rapid communications from the field to decision-making managers make procrastination an obsolete, and even dangerous, leadership trait.

Erratic Behavior

Of grave concern is volatile behavior that is inconsistent with a market situation. Employees can understand the need for a flexible managerial style or even a certain amount of unconventional behavior, if it is understood and accepted as part of a manager's inherent personality. However, they are unable to tolerate inconsistency and sudden erratic mannerisms, particularly if there is no apparent reason for what could be perceived as chaotic behavior. (See Table 3.4, Why Morale Suffers.)

Table 3.4. Why Morale Suffers

- Employees are often skeptical of management's true commitment to meaningful change.
- The work environment does not encourage innovative thinking.
- Employees have little or no confidence that their opinions and ideas will be given any meaningful attention – with the likelihood that they will be dismissed without explanation.
- Demotivators exist, such as job boredom, unfairness, casting blame, barriers to promotion, lack of recognition, and clamping down on mistakes.
- Managers fail to view self-esteem as a powerful motivator to move individuals forward. Also, individuals do not wish to pass for cowards in the eyes of their peers. (See Maslow's hierarchy list in Chapter 2.)
- Little effort is given to the dynamic influence of unity, which is established by discipline and leadership.

LEADERSHIP IN THE COMPETITIVE ARENA

Leadership demands calmness and patience in addition to the above skills. It also means examining how you personally react in a variety of competitive situations. As important, it means observing the behavior of your employees, particularly when pushed against hard-nosed rivals.

This understanding is vital and will impact your decisions, especially when faced with the critical choice between taking the most daring or the most cautious solution.

The essential point is this: The nature of modern day business thinking in a competitive arena requires decisive and bold action. To take bold action entails effective leadership with motivated and disciplined employees ready and willing to implement the strategy as a team.

Therefore, develop your own personal style of leadership. Do so by tailoring it to your character and personality. However, the key here is to be certain that your style harmonizes with your organization's prevailing culture, and, of course, with the competitive job at hand.

While leadership relies on basic tenets regarding the treatment of individuals and dedication to clear-cut objectives, it is not an off-the-shelf package created by someone else for you to adopt. That is, leadership is not a one-size-fits-all style.

It should vary with the strategy you develop and the type of workforce you manage. Accordingly, look closely at your own behavior and match it to the attributes mentioned in this chapter.

If your strategy is going to succeed, your subordinates are the ones who must convert it to action. Therefore, take note of your employees' behavior and look out for any of these ominous signs: *disorder, complaints, silence, confusion,* and *agitation* before, during, and after a competitive encounter.

Also notice if their feelings are anchored to the fear of losing pride, status, employment, as well as any other areas of friction.

As important, look for an effect such as losing face in the eyes of peers.

Finally, the following attributes will get you closer to creating opportunities by projecting an optimistic leadership style:

Interpersonal skills. These affect how you deal with people. Skills include coaching, counseling, motivating, and empowering. It is the ability to communicate your intent effectively, without impatience or anger. If you want your subordinates to be calm and rational under pressure, you must set the tone.

Conceptual skills. These enable you to envision business-building strategies. Such skills require sound judgment, as well as the ability to think creatively, reason analytically, and act ethically. It also means sensitivity to the group's shared set of beliefs, values, and assumptions about what is important.

Technical skills. These are job-related skills you must possess to accomplish all your assigned tasks and functions. Included here is a wide-ranging awareness consisting of (1) respect for the diverse backgrounds of your personnel, (2) responsiveness to the varied cultures of your markets, (3) sensitivity to the customs and traditions of the intermediaries and customers with whom you interact, and (4) insight into the culture and practices of your competitors.

Tactical skills. These apply to solving tactical problems, which include handing localized situations concerning the deployment of resources. Tactical skills combine with the above interpersonal, conceptual, and technical skills to achieve objectives.

In the next chapter we get into the details of joining your leadership capabilities to the strategies and tactics that create opportunities.

4

Create Competitive Strategies and Tactics

Headlines from the business press:

Google Targets Microsoft

The Internet company plans to build a new computer operating system and intends to attack Microsoft in virtually all its businesses.

Competitive response: Microsoft fights back by offering a free, Web-based version of its Office software.

Panasonic Reaches Wide with Appliances for Emerging Markets

The Japanese company wants a bigger share of sales in developing markets, but knows that its $1,200 large-screen plasma-display TV sets and $3,000 nano-technology refrigerators are beyond the reach of low-wage families.

The company is planning a new line of offerings that could include TVs for $50, air conditioners for $100, and washing machines in the $200 range.

Competitive response: Local bargain brands, with years of experience squeezing costs and working on paper-thin margins, are offering similar products at low prices.

TiVo Wants to Be the Google of Television

The upstart company popularized a technology that makes it routine for viewers to save TV shows on a hard drive so they could watch them later, as well as fast-forward through the commercials.

Now it threatens to disrupt the industry and competitors by trying to remake itself as the Google of television – helping viewers navigate the increasing volume of entertainment choices and by selling ads.

Competitive response: The cable companies counterattack by rolling out their own digital videorecorders and taking away subscribers from TiVo.

AT&T is Looking to Turn Mobile Access Into a Big Business

AT&T assembled a team to operate like a start-up. Mission: Come up with innovative ways for people to use its wireless network. Strategy: Go beyond cellphones and hook up all manner of electronics to the Internet – from digital cameras and navigation devices to parking meters.

Competitive response: Verizon and other rivals are pursuing similar avenues of growth and already have made a headstart by selling inexpensive netbooks and signing up customers to their networks.

What do those companies have in common[1]?

The actions and counteractions act out in aggressively disputed marketplaces where competing managers are pitted against each other. The endgame is measured by sales, market share, and profitability.

In addition to the hard numbers, managers' actions also aim to (1) protect their existing customers from rivals' take-over strategies and (2) prevent competitors from interfering with implementing their own business plans.

The essential point in all these examples: It is a manager's skillful application of strategies and tactics that will outwit, outfight, and outwin competitors and result in success.

1. Giving examples of large companies is valid if you consider that many big businesses consist of a group of smaller operations, such as divisions, departments, business units, or product lines. Each functions with its own budget, markets its own set of products to a defined customer segment, and faces a unique set of competitors. For funding, each operation presents a business plan to senior management, which serves as a "banker."

By mastering the rules of strategy, you will be able to survive the tough times, gain ground over competitors, and maintain a pathway to growth through opportunities. Therefore, it's in your best interest to gain a firm grasp on the roots of strategy, understand how to develop them, and know how to implement them.

What, then, is strategy? What are its origins? What are the universal principles of strategy that have stood the test of time where two or more rivals seek the same objective? And, most important, how can you apply strategies to help create opportunities in a competitive environment?

DEFINING BUSINESS STRATEGY

Strategy is a term freely used and applied to numerous functions of a business. While various definitions of strategy exist, the following will be used in this book:

Strategy is the art of coordinating the means (money, human resources, and materials) to achieve the ends (profit, customer satisfaction, and company growth) as defined by company policies and objectives.

In more pragmatic terms, strategy consists of actions to achieve objectives at three distinct levels:

First, *corporate strategy.* At this level, strategy is developed at the top echelon of the company. The aim here is to deploy resources through a series of actions that would fulfill the vision and objectives as expressed in the business plan.

Second, *mid-level strategy*. At this juncture, strategy operates at the department or product-line level. It is more precise than corporate strategy. Typically, it covers actions in a three- to five-year period and focuses on fulfilling specific objectives.

Also at this level, strategy embodies two-zones of activity: First, actions to create and retain customers; second, actions geared to preventing competitors from dislodging your company from its market position by seizing market share and customers.

Third, *lower-level strategy* – or tactics. This level requires a shorter timeframe from those at the two higher levels. Normally, it links with a company's or product line's business plan, marketing plan, and annual budget.

In everyday application, tactics are actions designed to achieve short-term objectives, while in support of longer-term objectives and strategies.

Also, tactics are precise actions that cover such areas as: pricing and discounts, advertising media and copy themes, the Internet, sales force deployment and selling aids, supply chain methods, customer relationship programs, training, product packaging, value-added services, and the selection of a market segment to launch a product.

ROOTS OF STRATEGY

Strategy doesn't have its roots in business applications. Its origins come from the ancient Greeks and is derived from the word strategia (or strategos), meaning to lead an army or generalship. Generals over the centuries have relied on military strategy to conquer territory and gain power.

That meant imposing their will on others and maximizing the impact of their economic and human resources to achieve their goals. The challenges: Outmaneuver competing forces, gain territory and power, and conserve resources while expanding their influence. While the terminology varies, these challenges are not much different from those of business.

To impose their wills on others, generals had to distract and unbalance their opponents physically and psychologically. Faced with a conflict of wills, the commanders on the battlefield were forced to maximize the effectiveness of their economic and human resources to achieve their goals.

Most confrontations – whether military, business, or even athletic – involve a defense protecting its ground and an offense trying to overtake that ground. The key to offensive strategy, therefore, is the efficient use of resources to accomplish the attack and overtake the territory – or in business terminology, secure a market.

Although the destructive aspects of war are not present in business, there is a reasonable parallel when you consider the demise of organizations, some global leaders; the layoffs of vast numbers of personnel; the closing of physical plants – as well as the severe economic impact and societal disruption that damages, and in many instances decimates, regions, cities, and local communities.

Thus, business scholars, executives, and line managers readily accept the comparisons and find practical wisdom in studying the chronicles of documented military strategies that span 2,500 years of recorded history. They serve as an excellent additional resource for business study, as opposed to relying only on a single dimension of examining current business practices with its limited time perspective.

The military viewpoint provides five primary strategy principles that can strengthen your understanding of strategy, which you can apply to meet most of your competitive challenges. These principles include direct attack, indirect attack, envelopment attack, bypass attack, and guerrilla attack.

PRIMARY STRATEGY PRINCIPLES

Direct Attack

> ***Key point:***
>
> No manager is justified in launching a sales and marketing campaign against a competitor who is entrenched in an actively defended market-leader position.

A direct attack should be avoided at all costs, especially so for the smaller business. Most often it results in exhausting budgets, demoralizing employees, and using hard to replace resources without achieving your objectives.

Even if you do achieve some minor objective, such as obtaining minimal sales or gaining a foothold in a market niche, few resources will remain for penetrating the market and realizing its full potential. Using the military parallel, no resources are available to "get off the beaches" before the opponent counter-attacks and succeeds in pushing them back "into the sea."

Support for the above assertions come from one of the most respected military historians of the twentieth century, B.H. Liddell Hart. In his authoritative book *Strategy*[2], the eminent British author presents a massive study covering 12 wars that decisively affected the entire course of European history in ancient times and 18 major wars of modern history up to 1914. In all, these 30 conflicts embraced more than 280 major military campaigns, and spanned 2,500 years.

The study revealed that in only six of those campaigns did a decisive result follow a direct frontal attack. And of those six, most began with an indirect attack but were changed to a direct attack due to a variety of battlefield conditions.

Consequently, Liddell Hart states:

"History shows that rather than resign himself to a direct approach a Great Captain will take even the most hazardous indirect approach – if necessary over mountains, deserts or swamps with only a fraction of his force even cutting loose from his communications. He prefers to face any unfavorable condition rather than accept the risk of frustration inherent in a direct approach."

Thus, reviewing the overwhelming evidence of history, we can conclude the following:

1. No general is justified in launching his troops in a direct attack upon an enemy who is firmly in position.
2. In like manner, we can interchange the above terms and state with strong confidence that no manager is justified in deploying sales, marketing, and other resources in a direct

2. B.H. Liddell Hart, *Strategy* (New York: Praeger, 1954).

campaign against a competitor who is firmly entrenched in an actively defended market-leader position.

3. Consequently, if there is little or no differentiation in such areas as product, promotion, pricing, or distribution – as perceived by the market – there is minimal chance of success.

Just how much stronger is the defense against a direct attack? The military genius Napoleon estimated that a three-to-one advantage was needed to break through a defender's line in a direct frontal attack. In Napoleon's time, a three-to-one advantage meant having three times more infantry, artillery, and cavalry, as well as employing three times more logistical support than was available to the defender. Therefore, even if a breakthrough did occur by using a massive infusion of resources, inadequate human and material resources would remain for follow-up and penetration.

Key point:

The use of a direct frontal attack against an entrenched competitor is a sign of a mediocre manager.

In business terms, a three-to-one advantage translates into three times more salespeople, advertising expenditures, product development, logistical, and administrative support, which is a huge expenditure of resources for little, or perhaps, no return. This condition is especially troublesome for the small and mid-size firm.

A classic business example of a direct attack is **General Electric, RCA**, and **Xerox** launching a direct frontal attack against the formidable **IBM**, an entrenched defender of its computer market. Early on, those companies attempted to penetrate IBM's active defenses with an undifferentiated product. RCA alone lost $500 million on the venture. All three attackers retreated from that market.

To add an historical perspective to the negatives of the direct attack, the renowned General Douglas MacArthur of World War II fame stated at a strategy meeting, "The use of a direct frontal attack is a sign of a mediocre commander and there is no room in modern warfare for such a commander."

To paraphrase MacArthur for your purpose:

The use of a direct frontal attack against an entrenched competitor is a sign of a mediocre manager and there is no room in today's competitive environment for such a manager!

Indirect Attack

> ***Key point:***
>
> An indirect attack relies on differentiation and concentrates on market segments that are emerging, neglected, or poorly served by competitors.

If the direct attack requires the aggressor to expend an enormous quantity of resources, thereby depriving it of strength for further market penetration, then an alternative approach must do the opposite. Such an approach is to place the competitor at a disadvantage by concentrating on its weaknesses.

According to Liddell Hart, the indirect attack is the most fruitful approach. It has the greatest chance of success while conserving the greatest amount of strength.

Application

When an indirect attack is applied as a business strategy, the attacker concentrates on a weakness in those market segments that are emerging, neglected, or poorly served by competitors. Such a segment is the initial *point of entry*.

What follows the entry is the selection of strategies. For instance, strategies could consist of a *product* (a handheld electronic unit that hooks up all types of devices to the Internet), *price* (TVs, washing machines, refrigerators affordable for emerging markets), *promotion* (using the Internet to help viewers navigate through product and pricing choices), or *distribution* (bypassing retail outlets and providing books through video devices.) Refer to Chapter 6, Table 6.1, Creating Problem-Solving Strategies, for a comprehensive list of possibilities.

Once entrenched in the initial market segment and able to establish market presence, a customer base, and a supply chain network, the attacker can more easily secure additional parts of the market previously dominated by competitors. This critical follow-up to entry is called market expansion.

Classic examples

Examples abound of the advantages of the indirect attack in business. For instance:

- German and Japanese automakers first entered the North American automobile market with small cars, a market neglected by domestic manufacturers during the 1970s and poorly served during the 1980s and beyond.
- **Miller** discovered the light beer segment as an emerging market.
- **Honeywell** concentrated its computers at the medium- and small-sized cities initially unattended by IBM.
- **Apple** became a dominant factor in schools early on, specifically serving that segment with computer hardware and software, also left vacant by IBM.
- **Wal-Mart** originally opened its stores in towns with populations under 2,500, ignored at that time by the leading retailers.

With the abundance of business examples and with evidence from military history, there is never any justification to undertake a direct frontal attack in today's competitive market. Rather, it is your obligation and necessity to use an indirect approach to:

1. Find opportunities in unattended, poorly served, or emerging market segments. (See Chapter 7, 'Segment Your Markets'.)
2. Create a competitive advantage by using your product/service, price, promotion, and distribution in a configuration that cannot be easily matched by competitors. Then apply your maximum strength against the weaknesses of your opponent.
3. Mobilize all your available resources on fulfilling the unmet needs and wants of the selected market. Then work diligently at solidifying relationships with your customers for the long-term.
4. Expand into additional segments of the market in a planned, deliberate approach that keeps in mind the overwhelming advantages of the indirect approach.

Envelopment Attack

An envelopment strategy consists of two stages:

- First, beginning as an indirect attack, the attacker focuses on a specific market segment for a point of entry.
- Second, by identifying additional market segments and adding new products, the attacker then uses an expansion strategy to *envelop* the entire market.

In the consumer market, for example, **Seiko** illustrates the indirect-envelopment combination. The company initially entered the watch market in one segment, digital watches, and then enveloped the overall market by offering as many as 400 models of watches to penetrate every major watch outlet and customer segment, overwhelming their competitors.

In the industrial sector, **Timken** offers 26,000 shaped ballbearing combinations, a product line unmatched by any competitor. The company thereby enveloped that market segment and fulfilled practically all its customers' needs in that product category.

> ***Key point:***
>
> To envelop the entire market, the attacker uses an expansion strategy by identifying additional market segments and adding new products.

Bypass Attack

The *bypass attack* allows the attacker to circumvent its chief competitors and diversify into unrelated products or unrelated geographical markets for existing products.

For example, **Eastman Kodak** successfully used a bypass approach into such diverse areas as electronics and biotechnology, with products as diverse as electronic publishing systems, cattle feed nutrients, and anticancer drugs.

However, this relatively sudden move into diverse fields followed an ultraconservative period in which Kodak temporarily stalled and competitors grabbed such markets as instant photography, 35mm cameras, and video recorders. All of which were natural extensions of Kodak's core business.

The bypass strategy does include a measure of risk because expansion into a range of unrelated fields can diminish a company's strength in any single area.

> ***Key point:***
>
> The bypass strategy includes some risk that can diminish a company's strength in any single area.

Guerrilla Attack

Guerrilla attack involves small intermittent attacks on different markets. It is useful for a small company competing against a large corporation, or where a product with a small market share is struggling against a brand leader.

Guerrilla attacks are characterized by a number of actions: selective price cuts, supply interferences, executive raids, intensive promotional bursts, and assorted legal actions. The aim is movement and surprise to create confusion and distraction, and to cause the opposing manager to make mistakes.

STRATEGY APPLICATIONS

The military-business connection can be summed up in the following parallel statements:

The object of war is a better state of peace.
B.H. Liddell Hart

The object of business is to create a customer.
Peter Drucker

With an understanding of the roots of strategy, we can now go beyond the vast historical perspective and focus on strategy applications for business. These can be condensed into five primary applications that are characteristic of all well executed strategies – practical principles that you can use to grow your business.

These applications consist of speed, indirect approach, concentration, alternative objectives, and unbalancing competition. A thorough understanding of these practical guidelines is critical if you are to implement business-building strategies and create opportunities.

Below, you will find descriptions of the strategy guidelines, examples from actual corporations, and step-by-step procedures for applying them to your firm.

Speed

An essential ingredient in applying competitive strategy is speed. There are few cases of overlong, dragged-out campaigns that have been successful. Exhaustion – the draining of resources – has killed more companies than almost any other factor. "Without exception, all of my biggest mistakes occurred because I moved too slowly," declared John Chambers, CEO of **Cisco Systems**.

Extended deliberation, procrastination, cumbersome committees, and indecisiveness are all detriments to success. Drawn out efforts often divert interest, diminish enthusiasm, the damage morale.

Employees become bored and their skills lose sharpness. As bad, the gaps of time created through lack of action give competitors a greater chance to create barriers that can blunt your efforts.

Therefore, it is in your best interest to evaluate, maneuver, and concentrate your marketing forces quickly to gain the most profit at the least cost, in the shortest span of time.

The following classic case illustrates these points:

Smirnoff vodka was a leading brand with a dominant share of the U.S. market. At one point, Smirnoff was attacked on price by another brand, Wolfschmidt, produced by **The Seagram Company Ltd**. Wolfschmidt was priced at $1.00 a bottle less than Smirnoff and claimed the same quality. The purpose of the price attack was to capture market share from Smirnoff.

Recognizing the real danger of customers switching to Wolfschmidt, Smirnoff managers quickly devised a three-part plan to protect its market dominance:

1. Raise the price of Smirnoff by $1.00 and preserve the premier image the brand already enjoyed.
2. Introduce a new brand, Relska, and position it head-to-head as a fighting brand against Wolfschmidt's price and market segment.
3. Introduce still another brand, Popov, at $1.00 less than Wolfschmidt.

By the end of the 1980s, Smirnoff remained number one of all imported and domestic vodka shipped in the U.S., with Popov in the number two position. Wolfschmidt did not achieve its objective of capturing market share. In fact there was some deterioration in the brand's share.

The proverbs "Opportunities are fleeting" and "The window of opportunity is open" have an intensified truth in today's markets. Speed is essential for gaining the advantage and exploiting the opportunity.

> ***Key point:***
>
> Speed is essential for gaining the advantage and exploiting the benefits.

Organizing for Speed and Quick Reaction

> ***Key point:***
>
> To make your effort effective, reduce the decision-making levels. The fewer the levels, the more dynamic the operations tend to become.

As a small company you should have the advantage of reacting with speed. This is especially applicable in these three areas:

First, new technologies in product development, communications, and especially with the Internet, you can react quickly and decisively at a pace faster than a large-size company.

Second, with a simplified system of control and typically with a short-decision-making chain, you can take advantage of new technology and be able to gather market intelligence.

Third, with a more flexible organization you hold a clear-cut opportunity to achieve greater market penetration. That is, with speed and flexibility you can adjust to varying market circumstances, come up with alternative objectives, and concentrate on your competitor's weak points.

Indirect Approach

As already noted, you should avoid the frontal attack at all costs in favor of an indirect approach, which can include any of the nondirect forms of attack – envelopment, bypass, or guerrilla.

The entire purpose of the indirect approach is to circumvent the strong points of resistance and concentrate in the markets of opportunity with a competitive advantage built around product, price, promotion, and distribution. This approach is especially appropriate for smaller organizations.

A classic example to illustrate the indirect strategy is the Japanese copier makers' entry into North America by attacking Xerox. Initially, the offshore companies avoided a direct approach of entering the market with large copiers, a market segment dominated by Xerox. Instead, they focused on the vacant small copier segment that was largely left unattended by Xerox.

Another early example is that of German and Japanese firms dominating the small automobile market in North America, further illustrating an indirect attack. Those companies selected a market segment that was emerging and then introduced a product line that avoided a direct confrontation with entrenched competitors.

Then, there is Amazon.com, which has become a legend in its own time by using the Internet and a vast selection of discounted and used book titles as an indirect approach to outflank most other booksellers. For expansion, Amazon moved into a vast collection of products to envelop many segments of the online market.

> ***Key point:***
>
> The object of the indirect approach is to circumvent the strong points of resistance and concentrate in the markets of opportunity.

Concentration

> ***Key point:***
>
> Concentration means focusing your strengths against the weaknesses of your competitor.

Concentration has two uses in strategy terms:

First, it means directing your full attention toward a market or customer group and fulfilling its specific needs and wants. In modern practice, concentration applies to target marketing, segmentation, and niche marketing.

Second, as applied to strategy, concentration means focusing your strengths against the weaknesses of your competitor.

How do you determine the competitor's weaknesses? Devote enough time to conducting a competitive analysis (see Chapter 6, 'Distinguish Your Business'). By detecting the strength – weakness relationship, you can then isolate the areas of competitive weakness and thereby determine where to apply your strength.

Application

To concentrate in a market, use as many of the following techniques as appropriate to your company's situation:

1. As with the indirect approach, identify your competitor's weaknesses and your company's strengths.
2. Concentrate on a market segment that you have determined represents growth and, in turn, could help launch you into additional market segments.
3. Introduce a differentiated product (or product modification) not already developed by existing competitors.
4. Seek multilevel distribution, such as private labeling your product for existing suppliers. Concurrent with that action, establish your own brand.
5. Therefore, if one strategy falters the alternative strategy often wins.

Follow-up by expanding into additional market niches with the appropriate products so you can envelop the entire market category, providing your firm has the resources to sustain the effort.

Alternative Objectives

There are three central reasons for developing alternative, or multiple objectives:

First, business plans generally call for fulfilling several long- and short-term goals. Therefore, a wide range of objectives are required with a variety of timeframes.

Second, alternative objectives permit enough flexibility to exploit opportunities as they arise. By designing a number of objectives, any of which can be used depending on the circumstances, you hold options for achieving one objective when others fail.

Third, and most important, alternative objectives keep your competitors in a predicament – unable to detect your real intentions. By displaying a number of possible threats, you force a competing manager to spread his resources and divert his attention to match your actions.

Since a major unpredictable factor is the human will (the mind of one manager against the mind of a competing manager), the intent of alternative objectives is to unbalance the opposing manager into making mistakes. These include: inaction, distraction, wrong decisions, false moves, or misinterpretation of your real intent. You thereby expose vulnerabilities that you can exploit through concentration of effort.

Key point:

Alternative objectives prevent competitors from detecting your real intentions.

Application

To use alternative objectives, follow these guidelines:

1. Consider such areas as customer service, improved delivery time, extended warranties, sales terms, after-sales support, packaging, and management training as sources of alternative objectives.
2. Identify alternative niches in the initial stages of market entry to cause your opposing manager to become distracted from your real intentions.
3. Exploit your competitors' confusion by concentrating your efforts on the weak spots that represent opportunities.

Unbalancing Competition

Key point:

Strategy's ultimate purpose: the reduction of resistance.

Victory in many competitive situations is not necessarily due to your brilliance, but to the mistakes of the opposing manager. If brilliance plays a roll at all, it is in your deliberate efforts to develop situations that unbalance your competition.

Those efforts, in turn, produce psychological and physical unbalancing effects on the opposing manager by means of speed, indirect approach, concentration, and alternative objectives. Moreover, unbalancing fulfills strategy's ultimate purpose: The reduction of resistance.

You might try an unbalancing action, for example, by announcing a new product that could make the competing manager's product line obsolete. Even a press release about a yet-to-be introduced service can "make them sweat" and create panic, and cause mistakes. This unbalancing is practiced continuously in day-to-day activities that range from the threat of legal action to the effects of joining forces with another rival.

Application

To unbalance competition, use these guidelines:

1. Identify those unique areas of your operation where your competitor is unable or unwilling to respond to your actions.
2. Make a conscious effort to create an unbalancing effect through surprise announcements, for example, of a new computerized ordering procedure, just-in-time delivery, or technical on-site assistance. The unbalancing effect will have the greatest impact to the extent that you are able to maintain secrecy until the last possible moment.
3. Utilize new technology to unbalance competitors and make them rush to catch up. Investigate the various technologies, such as interactive video systems and the pervasive uses of social networks on the Internet to enhance communications.

The following case example summarizes the concepts and techniques discussed thus far.

SAS, a software company with a total customer orientation, succeeds by devising strategies fine-tuned to customers' requirements, competitors' behaviors, industry trends, and environmental changes.

For instance, the company devised a series of moves to maintain momentum. SAS moved rapidly to:

- Design new software to profit from the business trend of establishing computerized relationships to link the complex networks in which most companies operate. One system calls for linking suppliers and customers by using unique software to track an entire industrial process from its starting point.
- Penetrate the numerous niches that make up the business-to-business markets. SAS broke its traditional policy of secrecy and revealed its proprietary codes to eager

developers, so they could create specialized applications software on a market-by-market roll out. The object: rapid deployment of software packages to gain a jump on such giants as Microsoft and Computer Associates.

- Modify its costly software into simpler, cheaper versions that provide financial, warehouse, and human resource packages for small and medium-size companies.
- Observe how some competitors may have stumbled in their product design or ability to market their offerings effectively. SAS then corrected the errors, launched its product with precision into targeted niches, and seized market share from competitors.

Key point:

Establish long-term bonding relationships with customers and suppliers, and work together for the profitable growth of your markets.

From the SAS case and the principles cited in this chapter, four major strategy lessons stand out:

First, while the tools of business (product development, marketing, distribution, financing) are physical acts, they are directed by a mental process. Meaning: Pay close attention to your customers, competitors, industry, and environmental trends. You will thereby be in an exceptional position to gain the upper hand against competitors, as you satisfy the needs of customers.

Second, the tougher you make your marketing practices, the more your competitors will consolidate against you. Result: You will harden the resistance you are trying to overcome. Even if you succeed in winning the market, you will have fewer resources with which to profit from the victory. Therefore, establish long-term bonding relationships with customers and suppliers, as you work together for the profitable growth of your markets. To repeat Peter Drucker's maxim, "The object of business is to create a customer."

Third, the more intent you are on securing a market entirely on your own terms, the stiffer the obstacles you will raise in your path. And the more cause competitors will have to try to reverse what you have achieved. Therefore, don't intentionally seek direct competitor confrontations. Doing so will exhaust resources and divert your attention from your customers' needs and problems. Instead, use the indirect approach.

Fourth, when you are trying to dislodge your competitor from a strong market position, leave that competitor a quick way to exit the market. Do so by increasing the gap between you and your competitor through product differentiation and value-added services.

A FOCUS ON COMPETITIVE STRATEGY TO CREATE OPPORTUNITIES

The five strategy applications: *speed, indirect approach, concentration, alternative objectives,* and *unbalancing the competition*, characterize the formation of competitive strategies and serve as the underpinnings for creating opportunities.

The following section further condenses them into just three fundamental components: *indirect approach, differentiation,* and *concentration*. Internalizing these principles will help you incorporate the strategy principles into a fine-turned actionable plan, thereby helping you devise competitive strategies to outperform competitors.

Indirect Approach

As discussed in the earlier section of this chapter as demonstrated in the SAS example, avoid a direct approach against an entrenched competitor. The odds are totally against you. Instead, where possible, take some of the following actions:

- Create confusion in the minds of opposing managers as to your real intentions in specific areas, such as time and place of product launch, pricing strategies, promotion campaigns, and types of differentiation.

- Search for unserved market segments and fill product gaps quickly in a way that preempts competitors and consequently gains a foothold in the selected segment with little or no opposition.
- Gain access to a supply chain through add-on services or special inducements.
- If appropriate, use legal actions or other unorthodox approaches to dislodge a competitor.

In all actions use speed to create surprise, which in turn will cause confusion among your competitors. Then use alternative objectives to further reinforce the dilemma in your competitor's mind about your intentions.

Differentiation

> ***Key point:***
>
> Although your product may seem like an indistinguishable commodity, there are always ways to differentiate it.

The most effective means of applying the indirect approach is to seek differentiation. (See Chapter 6, 'Distinguish Your Business'.) It is important to remember that even if your product may seem like an indistinguishable commodity, there are always ways to differentiate it.

Writes former Harvard Professor Theodore Levitt: "There is no such thing as a commodity."[3] His suggestions for differentiating products and services are summarized as follows:

Consider differentiation in such tangible areas as customer service, improved delivery time, extended warranties, sales terms,

3. Theodore Levitt, *The Marketing Imagination* (New York: The Free Press, 1983), p. 72.

after-sales support, packaging, and management training of your own staff and that of your distributors.

Also, try differentiation with such intangibles as reliability, image, nice-to-do-business-with reputation, credibility, prestige, convenience, value, responsiveness to problems, and access to key individuals in your firm.

While the competitive products may be identical, the suggested areas of differentiation add up to a total product package that moves you away from the commodity status and gives you a competitive edge, with the added potential for premium pricing.

Concentration

Your ability to implement concentration is predicated on the effective applications of the indirect approach and differentiation. Concentration is successful to the extent that you can distract the competitor and seek out an opportunity in an unserved, emerging, or neglected market segment. Concentration is also effective only to the extent that you can differentiate yourself from the competitor.

This particular component is so vital to successful strategies that Liddell Hart indicated that if all of strategy could be summed up into one word, it would be concentration.

You can apply those three fundamentals of strategy only if adequate competitive analysis is used. For example, identifying emerging markets is useful if you can preempt your competition and satisfy the needs and wants of those markets.

Or, employing areas of differentiation is advantageous to the extent that the competitors cannot, or are not willing to respond, to your action. The confidence level of your strategy is strengthened by your diligent efforts in using competitor analysis to shape an indirect approach.

POWER-UP YOUR BUSINESS STRATEGY: THE HUMAN TOUCH

During unpredictable market conditions, it is possible to accomplish much more with your staff than you would ordinarily consider feasible during easier times. In fact, the more you ask of your employees, the more likely you will get what you call for.

Within the framework of applying the human touch to strategy, use the following guidelines to help you assess your leadership skills and your staff's performance.

Begin with the following questions:

- How well have our employees been directed during the active part of a campaign, or at a particularly difficult competitive encounter?
- Were there intervals of confusing and misunderstood directions?
- Did our key personnel help or hinder good communications among those who had to implement the strategies?
- Were our personnel adequately briefed about the big picture? Or was it necessary to hold back information, or limit the detail about the full business plan?
- Was there a point at which certain individuals tended to quit the effort or simply become disinterested? In contrast, was there evidence of others moving forward?
- At what point in the control of employees, or in overseeing the general market situation, did we feel events slipping from our hands?
- Was there a time when we thought it was no longer possible to recover a position?
- What signs, signals, or systems could have alerted us to such an outcome and provided time to salvage the situation?
- Where and when did we resume control – if at all?

The major lesson from the above assessment is that you must use your creative imagination, training, and experience to prepare yourself to work in an unstable economic environment. It is a mode in which your eyes cannot always see, your best deductive powers cannot always fathom, and where you rarely can become completely familiar with a jumble of market events.

Your one remedy: Cultivate positive imagination as an essential ingredient of your skill-set and an integral part of staff training. The ability to form accurate mental pictures of a situation quickly is especially important to sort out conflicting actions.

Conversely, uncontrolled imagination can be disastrous. That is, if you fail to see events as potential opportunities, your mind leads you to form negative conclusions.

However, imagination is not a fanciful exercise in freefall. Enhance it with all the leadership qualities listed above and in Chapters 1 and 2. Then attach it to the core strategy rules discussed in the following chapters.

If you train yourself to manage the ongoing pressures of competitive encounters with discipline, with positive imagination to see you through the inevitable fog of uncertainty, and with business plans firmly attached to the strategy rules discussed thus far, you can turn even minor defeats into major victories.

What you don't want to do is develop actions that are mere repeats of yesterday's strategies, where you replay your hand for competitors to see and react to. This also leads to negative financial results, lowers employee morale, and loses unrecoverable resources.

However, it is appropriate to feed off the hard-earned lessons of past market campaigns. Find out what worked, didn't work, and what could be salvaged for next-generation strategies.

Also, in general terms, you want to align strategies with your organization's physical capabilities, your staff's skills and abilities, the company's history, its sensibility to competitive clashes, and modes of behavior.

Expressed succinctly: How does your strategy match-up with the company's culture? Giving attention to those areas differentiates your firm and gives it a special uniqueness.

Allied to these overall rules, is the importance of maintaining ongoing competitive intelligence. If you know your competitor's moves, you can determine with some accuracy which strategies will likely succeed and reject those with little chance of success.

As for your employees, your aim is to lift their morale and encourage their trust by instilling discipline and training to prevent them from caving-in against tough competitive situations. As the leader, you are still the decisive component in any strategies you create.

Also, try to avoid excessive caution that can result in loss of momentum, initiative, and a winning spirit. Finally, your aim is to foster team solidarity that inspires innovation. For anything significant to happen, it is your mind, as well as the unity of team effort, that produces a meaningful effect.

5

Decode Your Competitors

"Next to knowing all about your own business, the best thing to know is all about the other fellow's business."

John D. Rockefeller

Decoding competitors means becoming totally familiar with your rivals' way of thinking, including their value systems and style of management. Also, you want to understand how they operate, which means an awareness of the types of strategies they pursue, e.g., passive or aggressive. (See following information on types of competitors.)

The essential point: You want to acquire enough ongoing business intelligence, which can spell the difference between success and failure in creating opportunities.

Consequently, given the scope of information required to develop opportunities and strategies, it's up to you to look at a competitor with a 360-degree view. Using a circular approach will open your eyes to a changing marketplace of evolving technologies, environmental trends, and shifting buying patterns among your customers.

Also, in this panoramic scene you will be guided with information and insight that can impact your decisions about selecting markets, launching new products and services, and devising winning strategies.

That is why sales reps should be a starting point for gathering, examining, and acting on business intelligence at the field level, which includes giving special attention to competitors' current and likely moves.

Doing so will provide first-hand, on-the-ground data about competitive behavior under a variety of market conditions. Such information permits you to get a closer look at competitors' natural cultural patterns. It's all part of the decoding process.

Whether or not you have funds to conduct formal market research, you should still get actively involved in doing your own grassroots, hands-on competitive intelligence. You will then be more informed and better prepared to move quickly when presented with an opportunity. Here's what to look for:

- Observe changes in the character of your markets. Define your customers by demographic and behavioral characteristics. For instance, look for unmet customer needs that would enable you to respond rapidly in the form of products, services, methods of delivery, credit terms, or technical assistance.
- Maintain an ongoing dialogue with your customers to find out their most troublesome problems and frustrations. Meet salespeople, travel with them, if possible. Draw them out about what they see happening in their respective sales territories. Gain from their insights. It makes you and them more focused and able to react.
- Watch for competitors' alternative and substitute products that could replace your products or services. Examine customer usage patterns. Also observe deviations in regional and seasonal buying patterns. Check for changes from past purchase and usage practices that could translate into opportunities.
- Observe originality in selling, especially with the pervasive use of the Internet. Tune-in to current trends in promotional allowances, selling tactics, trade discounts, rebates, point-of-purchase opportunities, or seasonal/holiday requirements. Here, again, stay close to salespeople for such information.

- Examine your supply chain and look for opportunities to customize services consistent with the characteristics of the segment. Pay attention to warehousing (if applicable) and what could be fertile possibilities to innovate, such as electronic ordering and computerized inventory control systems that link to data mining capabilities.
- Search for innovations and product-line extensions to maintain an ongoing presence in your existing markets, or to gain a foothold in an emerging segment. Also look for ways to harness new technologies that lead to cost-effective and efficient operations. Doing so would make your company more competitive and result in broadening your customer base.

Key point:

Get involved in doing your own grassroots competitive intelligence. You will then be prepared to move quickly on an opportunity.

TYPES OF COMPETITORS

The eminent business scholar, Professor Philip Kotler[1] characterizes competitors as follows:

- Laid-back competitor: A competitor that does not react quickly or strongly to a rival's move.
- Selective competitor: A competitor that reacts only to certain types of attacks and not to others.
- Tiger competitor: A competitor that reacts swiftly and strongly to any assault on its terrain.
- Stochastic competitor: A competitor that does not exhibit a predictable reaction pattern.

1. See Philip Kotler's excellent book, *Marketing Management*, 11th Edition (Prentice Hall, New York 2003.)

The cultural signature of the competitor is a contributing factor in deciding, for instance, when you should enter a new market segment – if at all. In particular, decoding the cultural character of your rival is a vital factor when confronting a larger and more formidable competitor. It directly impacts which market you select, how and when to confront your competitor, and what considerations you give to the changing dynamics of markets.

Therefore, combining customers' needs and a competitor's profile into your conscious thinking represents the core ingredients for formulating your business strategy. You thereby are in an optimum position to create opportunities.

Consequently, it is your mandate to familiarize yourself with the inner workings of both your organization and that of your primary competitor.

Think about one of your more serious clashes with a competitor. At what point before, during, or after the encounter could you answer any of the following questions with a fair degree of accuracy?

About the competitive problem:

- When and how did you receive the first signal about your competitor's aggressive moves?
- At what point did you fully grasp the seriousness of what the competitor could possibly do to your market position?
- Who noticed the first signs of a problem: an experienced executive, a sales rep, or a novice manager? Looking back, how accurate was the assessment?
- How confident were you of its reliability? Did you consider the assessment useful enough to commit company resources?

About your competitor's performance:

- If your competitor's strategy failed, at what point in the unfolding action did you begin to see his efforts come apart?
- Did the competitor leave the market, mount an all-new effort, or retreat to his starting position?

- What were the telltale signs of weakness that caused the competitor's poor performance?
- Did the strategy fail because of insufficient financial or physical resources, lack of trained and experienced personnel, weak leadership, or faulty implementation?

About your company's performance:

- If the competitor was successful, at what point did your own situation unravel?
- Did the competitor catch you by surprise?
- What specifically was the nature of the competitor's strategy that caused your failed performance?
- Was it a case of insufficient reserves, manpower, budget, or back-up support? Or did you wait too long to react?
- On the other hand, if your efforts were successful, did you do an after-action report to determine how you succeeded, in what timeframe, under what conditions?
- When exactly was the turning point that assured your success?
- Was there an instance where events could have gone awry because of insufficient intelligence?
- How did your personnel hold up during the action?
- What lessons did you learn about your staff, your strategies, and the reliability of your competitive intelligence from the unfolding events?
- Would they be considered as topics for formal training or informal discussions at meetings?

The point of these questions: When immersed in a tough competitive encounter, you may not be fully acquainted with the overall strategies and short-term actions of your competitor. Or, for that matter, you may not be totally clear about your own strengths and vulnerabilities. Such doubts could include the capabilities of your personnel to perform under adverse conditions.

And that's not surprising. Trying to predict the performance of individuals at a particular time and during a special experience is loaded with uncertainties. Individuals blinded with fear and apprehension hinder calm and factual assessments, which often fill reports with inaccuracies. Also, people tend to believe evil rather than good. Consequently, what you get is feedback tainted with bad news and false dangers.

Even with what you believe is reliable intelligence, the moment you begin carrying out your plans, a thousand doubts may arise about the dangers and pitfalls that could develop.

Invariably, the situation affects you, too. Gnawing misgivings can creep into your mind about being seriously mistaken in your estimates of the situation. Such feelings of uneasiness often take hold. And from uneasiness to indecision are small, scarcely discernible steps.

What are the underlying issues that trigger such active thinking and sub-conscious feelings? Are they doubts about the competitor's strength, exaggerated estimates of its size, and concerns about the accuracy of the information?

And specifically, what about those individuals gathering and reporting the intelligence? As indicated above, individuals by nature are inclined to be timid and tend to overstate danger. Or, as likely, they steer toward self-interest as their prime motivation.

All those issues can weigh heavily on your mind and leave a misleading impression of your rival's intentions and capabilities. From that mindset arises a new source of indecision.

In spite of those complexities, you cannot take uncertainty as a reason for indecision, or as a rationale to forego action. Your best bet: Prepare as best you can by elevating competitive intelligence to the highest level. Make it an embedded part of your strategy development and its implementation.

Key point:

Prepare as best you can by elevating competitive intelligence to the highest level.

COMPETITIVE INTELLIGENCE: THE UNDERPINNINGS OF OPPORTUNITIES

The central idea behind competitive intelligence (CI) is this: If you know your rival's plans and are able to monitor his moves, then you can estimate with some degree of accuracy which strategies are likely to succeed and reject those with minimal chances of success. You can also assess the level of risk associated with going after an opportunity.

Further, with CI you can define your competitor's operating patterns. You can determine his market position, deployment of personnel, and where you are likely to face the most or least opposition. Knowing where your competitor's strength is formidable and where it is weak gives you lead time to take counteractions.

What better way is there to establish personal credibility for your managerial skills than being able to motivate your staff to handle potential threats and opportunities?

Therefore, CI, as an information-gathering, decision-making tool, affects all operating parts of your business either directly or indirectly. It is the centerpiece of all offensive and defensive actions. By exposing strengths and weaknesses in your situation, as well as in those of your competitors, CI functions as the core component when developing your plans.

If utilized with the same care you would give to a delicate instrument, CI can signal subtle changes in the marketplace. For instance, it can help you preempt and outmaneuver competitors, preserve financial expenditures for exploiting the best opportunities, and even protect your firm's secrets from inquisitive onlookers.

Therefore, listen to the incoming intelligence and be sure to evaluate the reliability of each source. Then, you can validate or disprove reports. In either case you gain confidence and become more adept at making accurate decisions.

The Call to Action

After you have assembled reliable intelligence and carefully deliberated on all that is meaningful, develop and implement your strategy with speed. It would be a far greater error to wait for a situation to clear up entirely. The reality of working in a dynamic competitive marketplace is that decisions are required – even in the fog of uncertainty.

Therefore, feel assured that the competitive intelligence you have assembled and screened, and the assessments you have made, will produce the results you expect. And even in the penetrating light of reality, should you discover that some intelligence is contradictory, false, or doubtful, then you have little recourse but to lean heavily on your judgment and move on.

That means: Depend on your knowledge of the industry, trust in your years of experience, show confidence in those key individuals with whom you work, recognize the value of your formal and informal training, and rely on the richness of your intuition.

Taking it a step further, should pangs of doubt still persist, yet intuitively you know that rapid action is called for if you are to prevent a potentially bad situation from deteriorating further, then tell yourself that nothing is accomplished without shifting to the offensive. Meaning: The only reason to pause or even retreat from a situation is to make preparations to eventually move forward.

> ***Key point:***
>
> Listen to the incoming intelligence and be sure to evaluate the reliability of each source.

Also, take comfort in this reality:

The risk is quite low that your best thought-out decision would easily ruin your company, provided you have gathered reliable competitive intelligence, followed the rules of indirect strategy, speed, and concentration. And, if all your planning is kept within a mask of secrecy, the competition will not see where you are going. (See Table 5.1.)

Table 5.1. Questions You Should Ask of Competitive Intelligence

- What is my competitor's overall business strategy, particularly where it impacts my plans?
- What is my competitor's financial picture, including breakdowns of costs and sales by product lines?
- What new products or services are under development?
- What new markets are expected to be targeted?
- How are the competitor's business units staffed and organized, especially in sales and product development?
- What is the caliber of the competitor's leadership?
- What market positions or market shares are held within each product segment?
- Where are the competitor's vulnerabilities by product depth, product quality, customer service, price, distribution, and reputation?

TOOLS AND TECHNIQUES OF COMPETITIVE INTELLIGENCE

Different types of tools and techniques are available for competitive intelligence. The following list itemizes the primary techniques. Select the ones based on the time and resources available to you. In any case, make every effort to use as many techniques as possible.

Sales Force

If you can work with a sales force, either your own or a distributor's reps, gather relevant data from these frontline individuals. Talk with them. Travel with them. They are in continuing contact with customers and are one of the prime sources of real-time intelligence.

To maximize their output, instruct them on what to observe and brief them on the reasons for doing so. That may involve sharing some information about your business plans. Also show them why competitive intelligence is the critical underpinning of all business strategy and a prime source of fresh opportunities.

A highly useful approach is to require call reports after all customer visits. While product usage, future sales prospects, and similar information are the usual topics reported, get them involved in adding specific facts about potential market opportunities.

Find out about strengths and weaknesses of competitors, significant changes in their strategies, and all other relevant activities. Be certain you read and react to their reports. The last thing sales reps want to hear is that their information is not being read or even acknowledged.

Customer Surveys

If budgets allow, use an outside market research organization to track competitors' activities. The investment could have a big payoff for you. However, if you cannot use a professional organization, try some of the following surveying techniques on your own:

In-person interviews: Question individuals with the aim of gaining insights about competitors. Such questioning could reveal gaps that can convert into opportunities. Those interviewed could be users of your product or service, competitors' sales reps, and distributors.

Telephone interviews: These interviews are somewhat difficult to secure with the prevalent use of voicemail and a variety of electronic devices. However, if handled by individuals who can gain the interviewees' attention because of their reputation, or by trading-off hard-to-find information, then this technique could be good source of information.

Mail interviews: Survey questionnaires are useful to acquire product information about competitors' products and services. In such instances, you can avoid using your company name. Instead, use the name of a generic-sounding research organization. In such research, and depending on the type of product, it is useful to offer a financial incentive for taking the time to fill out the questionnaire.

In one instance, a survey conducted by a publisher of trade magazines found to its surprise that there was very little overlap between its magazine subscribers, trade show attendees, and website users. Discovering that its audiences are significantly larger than the subscriber lists opened up a high-value opportunity that steered its strategy and allocation of marketing funds.

Published Data

Tap into the numerous sources of published information, from small-town newspapers where even a competitor's minor activities could make frontpage headlines, to trade journals that provide financial and product information about competitors.

Monitor want ads in print and over the Internet for clues to the types of personnel and skills being sought.

Look at the growing number of databases, etc., that provide voluminous quantities of competitive information. Some of these databases are free and available through public libraries; others are available at affordable costs.

If your competitors are public corporations, refer to their easy-to-access and information-crammed annual reports. With great detail, they reveal financial data, product development plans, and markets they view for future growth.

Allied to published data are the speeches by senior executives of competing companies. They offer valuable insights into their firms' future plans, industry trends, and strategies. At times it is astonishing how much sensitive information is provided in speeches that are given at trade shows and professional meetings.

Government Agencies

Depending on your location, you can access an ample supply of information from government sources through direct access, service organizations, or over the Internet. These sources usually include a vast amount of data from national, regional, and local government offices. Most information is available simply for the asking, or at modest cost.

In some instances information is available about types of work contracts previously awarded and to whom. Also, competitive information may be obtainable about the companies that are currently bidding for new contracts, which provides valuable clues to the type of competitors eligible to bid.

Industry Studies

Management consultancies, universities, trade associations, individual consultants, and investment securities firms conduct industry studies. Also, specialized companies publish industry and competitive information, such as:

- Data on a vast variety of products sold through retail outlets, television, magazines, and online.
- Weekly family purchases of consumer products and information on home food consumption by geographic and demographic breakdown.
- Reports of warehouse withdrawals to food stores in selected market areas.
- Statistics on television and radio markets according to demographics, experiential lifestyles, and brand preferences.

On-site Observations

You can handle this form of competitive intelligence personally. For instance, simply observing numbers of service vehicles and supply trucks in and out of a plant or at store locations provides first-hand information about the level of activity at a competitor's location.

In one case, an observer noticed several freight cars at a competitor's railroad siding. However, on closer examination, there was a barely visible layer of rust on the tracks, which indicated little or no recent rail activity. The observer concluded that the freight cars were there as a deliberate deception.

Also observing the schedules of employees arriving and leaving work can indicate patterns from which you can make reliable assessments. Even watching the movements of individuals in a parking area, the body language of people talking, or the work materials being carried can give clues that further fit an overall pattern.

As for a retail store environment, watching and recording individuals entering and exiting, with or without packages, could provide valuable information when compared to similar locations.

Competitive Benchmarking

Benchmarking is an assessment tool to compare and measure your firm's business processes against those of your competitors. Use it to reexamine your operation and reassess your business strategies and tactics.

The value of this tool is that you learn how and why some competitors perform with greater success than other organizations inside and outside your industry. You will find such information highly useful when planning strategies and determining which actions are likely to succeed.

Xerox Corporation is an outstanding example of successful benchmarking. The company developed the following 12-step process for competitive benchmarking.

Competitive Benchmarking

Planning

1. Identify benchmark outputs.
2. Identify best competitors.
3. Determine data collection methods.

Analysis

4. Determine current competitive "gap".
5. Project future performance levels.
6. Develop functional action plans.

Implementation

7. Establish functional goals.
8. Implement specific actions.
9. Monitor results and report progress.
10. Recalibrate benchmarks.
11. Obtain leadership position.
12. Integrate processes fully in business practice.

> ***Key point:***
>
> Benchmarking is a valuable tool to measure your firm's processes against those of your competitor.

Table 5.2 summarizes the benefits of benchmarking.

Table 5.2. Benefits of Competitive Benchmarking

• Improves your understanding of customers' needs and sensitizes you to the underlying competitive dynamics operating within your industry. • Helps you document why some competitors can perform similar processes at higher performance levels than at your organization. • Creates a sense of urgency to develop long-term objectives and strategies. • Encourages a spirit of competitiveness so that personnel recognize that performance levels in best-in-class organizations may exceed their own perceptions of what constitutes industry – and world-class – competitiveness. • Motivates individuals to new heights of innovative thinking and achievement.

INTERNAL COMPETITIVE INTELLIGENCE

The above techniques deal with the external environment, specifically the activities of competitors. Now, look internally at your own company's state of competitiveness and its ability to create new opportunities.

To get a complete picture of your organization, evaluate it by using the following approaches[2]:

- *Performance analysis* relates to your organization's structure and culture; employees' skills, morale, and discipline; internal procedures and systems; state of technology that drives resource utilization, product innovation, and productivity.
- *Strategy analysis* examines your firm's ability to react to aggressive competition, defend existing markets, and attack new markets. It also pertains to employees' capabilities to develop competitive strategies.
- *Strategic priorities analysis* concerns the long-term commitment to quality, customer orientation, and human resource development.
- *Cost analysis* relates to achieving competitive advantage and sustained profitability, which means looking at all business processes and determining when and where cost-cutting programs should be initiated.
- *Portfolio analysis* reviews markets and products and the strengths and gaps within each market segment.
- *Financial resource analysis* studies the availability of cash to support different competitive scenarios, which includes

---

2. There is an increasing use of dashboards in many companies. As information systems become more sophisticated, the ability to have an accurate collection of key performance indicators on a single page is now possible, and affordable, for most small- and mid-size companies. Dashboards can serve as the primary interface for measuring the success of an organization's strategy as part of a Business Performance Management (BPM) system.

initiatives to preserve product quality, maintain customer satisfaction, and provide ongoing technical and customer service.

- *Strength/weakness analysis* surveys your company's distinctive competencies and types of unique assets. The aim, here, is to determine sources for developing indirect strategies and how able you are to take on fresh opportunities. This analysis also includes more qualitative evaluations such as managerial leadership, employee attitudes and motivation, and the level of innovation in new product development.

Key point:

The aim of a strength/weakness survey is to develop indirect strategies and take on fresh opportunities.

Reverse Engineering

Here is where you gain the cooperation of technical, manufacturing, and financial personnel to breakdown competitive products to their component parts. Each part is identified on a range of criteria that covers manufacturing processes, utilization of current technologies, quality, performance, reliability, support services, and applications.

The product is then analyzed full cycle, including projections of costs, profits, return on investment, and any other financial measures that you use.

A side benefit of reverse engineering is that personnel representing most functions work together with the full awareness of customers' needs and the necessity to maintain a competitive lead. With some modification, reverse engineering works equally well with firms selling services.

MARKET SIGNALS

The competitive marketplace pulsates with the dynamics of competitive actions. When you tune-in to market signals, you gain invaluable insights to feed your own strategy process.

For instance, consider the following types of signals:

- A competitor abruptly announces a new value-added service. As important, the news triggers interest among your customers.
- A competitor introduces generous financial incentives for distributors to aggressively push their products, and your customers show strong signs of responding to the incentives.
- Unforeseen promotional bursts from competitors siphon-off sales you counted on.
- A competitor suddenly adds sales and service reps to a market segment that you thought was secure.
- An enhanced product quietly and suddenly introduced by a competitor to your customers begins to stir interest.

Then, there are other jarring signals that should alert you: Competitors open or close regional offices or plants. Sudden management changes are announced. New layoffs are revealed. Or upsetting rumors persist of new competitive alliances.

Not to be overlooked are the telltale signs of internal disorder and inept leadership as you observe competitors' personnel. For instance:

Managers openly show discouragement, display low morale, or exhibit short tempers. Sales reps overtly look for other jobs, criticize working conditions, or complain about shortages of sales aids and supplies.

They whisper about ineffectual leadership and cuts in wages. They whine about stringent rules restricting travel-related expenses. Or they object to executives excusing (or overlooking) abuses in corporate procedures.

At the same time, you may observe signs of general disorder, sloppiness, or indications of internal desperation. Those signals could represent changes in a competitor's traditional operating style, or patterns in handling customer relationships, or in the general demeanor of how executives interact with their personnel.

Also, look at the signals coming from customers who openly complain about a competitor's policies, rules, and procedures. And if pumped for detailed information, they often surge forward with a flood of grievances.

All these words and actions could indicate fear, uncertainty, insecurity, and a variety of deep-seated internal problems. It is in such a state of unbalance and discontinuity that you can spot opportunities.

Therefore, maintain an open two-way communications channel where signals from sales reps to management are red-flagged for priority handling.

One other area, usually apart from the general tools and techniques of competitive intelligence, and one worthy of a separate section, is the human side of competitive intelligence. More specifically, this entails employing *agents*.

> ***Key point:***
>
> Maintain an open two-way communications channel where signals from sales reps to management are red-flagged for priority handling.

EMPLOYING AGENTS

Agents are your eyes and ears at conferences, trade shows, and even at your competitors' locations. They go beyond the raw numbers, charts, surveys, benchmarking, and the other intelligence-gathering techniques.

They explore the human side of competitive intelligence by reporting on the behaviors and personalities of key individuals.

Their primary tool: personal interaction and observation. Agents also screen and interpret events, news, and validate or dismiss information gathered by other means.

Before moving forward and employing agents, however, observe a few general cautions:

First and foremost, make certain that you are not violating ethical and legal guidelines. And check if this approach agrees with your company's policies.

Second, assess prospective agents' motivations, personality traits, and talents. Then, you can determine in what capacity to employ them. For instance, some individuals' only interest is in money, with minor interest in obtaining accurate information about the competitor's true situation. In such cases, question their integrity and use great care in using them.

Third, develop a clear idea about the information you seek. Then make certain they understand what you want.

The following represents categories of agents, along with suggestions on how to use them.

Native Agents

Native agents are the types of individuals with whom you would normally interact during professional gatherings. They tend to voluntarily share company information to satisfy their personal interests, such as making new industry contacts and advancing their careers.

Often, they are somewhat uncaring about their respective company's security. Or they are simply not cautioned about the dangers of revealing company secrets.

You will find native agents in a variety of places: Trade shows serve as fertile venues for gathering intelligence from those individuals. It is also a place where competitors typically reveal extensive information through elaborate demonstrations about their products and freely distribute literature overflowing with facts about pricing, back-up services, logistics, product specifications, and so on.

Also, key individuals from competitors' organizations often present technical papers at open meetings, which detail sensitive information about upcoming products, services, and even market-entry plans. Then there is the Q&A period that usually follows where the speaker, trying to further impress an audience, pours out more information.

Another prime area for intelligence gathering is the familiar hospitality suite at trade shows and professional meetings where alcohol and talk flow freely. It's a spot where security is often lax and everyone's guard is down.

College classrooms represent another source of information, particularly where part-time instructors are also executives and use their respective companies as case examples. In some instances, where fellow students work in companies that interest you, useful data is often revealed about their companies through class presentations, term papers, and casual conversations.

Inside Agents

As with native agents, inside agents work for competitors. In many cases, they may have been bypassed for promotion, feel underpaid and underappreciated, relegated to an insignificant job, or generally pushed aside in a variety of political or power struggles within the organization.

They feel abused and see their careers languishing unless they make some bold move. They may also find themselves surrendering to financial pressures to sustain family and self. Their attitude may be now-or-never.

You need to assess such individuals carefully for their stability and determine how to use them judiciously. Obviously, you want their information within the bounds of ethical and legal guidelines.

Beyond personal observations, you would employ inside agents for their expertise to sort out meaningful information from scientific and professional journals, industry studies, or from innovative projects described in articles and professional papers written by the competitors' employees.

Product literature and product specification sheets readily available at trade shows and meetings are packed with tremendous detail. Your agents should be able to interpret the data for meaningful intelligence.

In-house company newsletters and news releases contain a fountain of information about individuals who left a competitor's employment and may have moved to the consulting circuit. If approached, these former employees may be willing to reveal information – unless specific contractual restrictions apply.

Press releases may include new employee announcements along with job descriptions, contracts and awards received, training programs available, office or factory openings or closures, as well as specific news that reveal competitor's activities. Here, again, your inside agent could handily provide useful interpretations.

Beyond the above listing, there is the continuing flow of rumors from customers and suppliers that your agent can sort out and verify. Additionally, there are local sources worth tapping, such as banks, local trucking companies, and real estate offices.

Double Agents

These agents try to extract intelligence about your company. Stay alert to their intentions. Once identified, you could attempt to turn them around and get them working on your behalf.

They would then serve in the same capacity as inside agents. Here, too, you can assume double agents seek lavish rewards and may even show similar personality traits and motivations as inside agents. However, it is in your best interest to exercise caution. That is, determine the sincerity of these individuals, the reliability of their information, and how long you can expect them to remain loyal to your cause. Once again, make certain you are not violating ethical, legal, or policy guidelines.

Expendable Agents

These agents are your own people who are deliberately fed inaccurate information, which is disseminated in a variety of ways to cause competitors to make wrong decisions. These contrived leaks take many forms.

For example, passing fabricated information about new product features through sales reps who come in contact with competitors' reps, or product managers revealing false dates about a product launch that would disrupt a competitor's plans.

In spite of your possible discomfort when undertaking such activities, look at the situation from strictly a strategist's viewpoint. Misinformation needs distribution to divert competitors from directly opposing your indirect strategy moves.

You thereby preserve your company's hard-won market position, control needless expenditures of financial and human resources fighting unnecessary market battles, and avoid disrupting your strategies.

> ***Key point:***
>
> Misinformation needs distribution to divert competitors from directly opposing your *indirect* strategy moves.

Living Agents

These agents usually provide the most credible information. They are generally experienced, talented, and loyal individuals who can gain access to, and become intimate with, a competitor's high-level executives. They sit in a position to learn their plans and observe movements. These individuals are truly the eyes and ears and often enjoy the closest and most confidential relationships.

Perhaps the one unsettling issue to cope with when using agents – but certainly worth knowing – is which of your employees knowingly or inadvertently passes on your company's information directly or indirectly to competitors. Eventually, those individuals are exposed and you can obtain valuable clues about what motivated them to those acts.

Another concern: Engaging in such stealth activities is usually contrary to the type of practices most managers care to undertake. Again, think of business intelligence as essential to running a company in a highly competitive environment. Above all, it is indispensable to the development and integrity of competitive strategies.

Table 5.3 summarizes the competitive intelligence process.

Table 5.3. The Competitive Intelligence 6-Step Process

1. Competitors' size: Categorize by market share, growth rate, profitability, as well as any other quantitative measures meaningful to your company and industry.
2. Competitors' objectives: Determine competitors' intentions related to product innovation, market leadership, global reach, regional distribution, and similar areas that would indicate a strategic direction.
3. Competitors' strategies: Analyze their internal strategies (speed of product development, manufacturing capabilities, delivery, and marketing expertise) and their external strategies (supply chain network, field support, market coverage, and aggressiveness in defending or building market share.)
4. Competitors' organization: Examine organizational design, culture, operating systems, internal communications, leadership, and overall caliber of personnel.
5. Competitors' cost structure: Check up on how efficiently they can compete, how long they can sustain pricing competition, the cost or difficulty of exiting a market, and their views about short-term versus long-term profitability.
6. Competitors' strengths and weaknesses: Identify areas vulnerable to a concentrated effort, as well as those strong areas that should be avoided.

COMPETITIVE INTELLIGENCE APPLICATIONS

From a strategy viewpoint, you can apply competitive intelligence in the following areas: Market selection, maneuver, and positioning.

All of these areas are primary components for cultivating opportunities.

Market selection

Beyond the standard segmentation groupings by demographic, geographic, and psychographic (lifestyle) criteria, use CI to highlight viable opportunities in markets with distinctive characteristics. For instance:

- Look for opportunities where you enjoy superior skills and resources to take a commanding lead in a market segment. That means latching on to new market and product trends, adapting online marketing methods to match new buying patterns, or finding ways to secure a solid position in the supply chain.
- Search for a segment where prospective customers' values, histories, and experiences match the unique characteristics of your company's products and services.

  Included here are markets that cater to those individuals sensitive to such topical issues as the "green" environment, weather, safety, pollution, government legislation, social movements, poverty, human rights, public opinion, workers' concerns, and economic matters.
- Try to find segments you possibly overlooked, or those that are poorly served. CI is valuable in helping you plug those segments before competitors can move in with their offerings and make your position untenable.

  In the normal course of keeping CI working for you, new opportunities can crop up at any time as you view the physical and psychological posture of your competitor. Therefore, keep in mind that marketplaces move and shift relentlessly and are subject to a variety of dynamic forces.

> ***Key point:***
>
> Market selection, maneuver, and positioning are primary components for cultivating opportunities.

Maneuver

Maneuver requires roundabout moves and secrecy. It means taking actions opposite of what your competitor might expect. Doing so avoids showing your hand to vigilant competitors. You also steer clear of direct confrontations, such as damaging price wars.

That is why you should rely on CI to make careful estimates about your (a) customers' buying patterns and (b) competitors' vulnerabilities. This combination is also known as two-zones of activity. Giving close attention to these zones helps you form more accurate estimates about the conditions that continually face you.

Yet, even with good intelligence, there are still the ever-present uncertainties when launching a new product or entering a previously unserved market. If you just repeat yesterday's strategies, then you just blunder ahead chasing a vague advantage with uncertain outcomes.

A better way is to use a process of *probe, penetrate,* and *exploit.*

Probe means making forays into test markets based on the competitive intelligence guidelines already indicated. Here's how it works:

First, deliberately probe for viable market segments and obtain feedback about consumer acceptance of your product or service. You would also use the probes to obtain feedback related to pricing, distribution, and promotion strategies in preparation for a full market rollout.

Or,

Second, you can skip market tests and rapidly mount a full-scale campaign, provided you have enough confidence in your research. Or you have evidence that a competitor's actions are going to interfere with your efforts if you wait for market tests to be completed.

Penetrate means expanding your presence in those segments initially identified in the market probes. Once you have located likely points for market entry, maneuvering takes over to avoid an outright confrontation with any opposing competitor.

Here is where you maximize your presence by locking up key customers, securing a workable position in the supply chain, and enriching your product and service offerings to satisfy the specific needs of customers.

Exploit suggests further maneuvering to obtain maximum advantage and increase market share through such strategies as differentiation and value-added services.

Positioning

Pioneered by Al Reis and Jack Trout during the 1980s, positioning was popularized as, "Not what you do to a product. Positioning is what you do to the mind of the prospect."

And from Professor Philip Kotler (Northwestern University), "Positioning is the act of designing the company offer and image so that it occupies a distinct and valued place in the target customers' minds."

Both definitions presuppose that a product's position results from securing a valued place early on in the mind of the prospect and, barring unforeseen circumstances, retaining that dominant position.

If positioning results from securing a valued place in the marketplace and in the prospect's mind, it comes about as the result of four influences, all of which are triggered by CI:

1. The image of your company, brand, or individual product, from which you can configure strategies and establish a growth-oriented market position.

2. The factors that drive the markets, which include the demographic and behavioral characteristics of your customers. For instance, **Panasonic** focused its expansion moves on emerging markets with cut-rate prices on TVs and refrigerators. The company used what it calls "lifestyle research" conducted by its local marketing teams to design products specifically designed for the target market.
3. Customers' perceptions of your products, services, and company. This information permits you to isolate what they like, dislike, and recommend changing.
4. Accurate information about your competitors, as discussed earlier.

Summarizing: From the opening moments of a product launch, or an effort to dislodge a competitor from a market segment, or a campaign to outmaneuver a market leader, everything is uncertain except what you intuitively sense and factually understand from competitive intelligence.

That combination is the only means you have for penetrating the fog that clouds competitive actions. It is all you have to decide how to manage your resources, direct your personnel, and activate your strategies.

While your instinctive feelings of what constitutes proper action are always present, what needs your continuous attention is a commitment to use every conceivable approach to obtain reliable competitive intelligence. You are then in the optimum situation to deal with the spontaneous market situations that require your best judgment when seeking opportunities.

6

Distinguish Your Business

At this point in the book, let's pull together the key points from the previous chapters, introduce the main ideas from the following chapters, then tie them into a set of *guidelines, rules,* and *applications* you can use to distinguish your business and create opportunities.

GUIDELINES TO DISTINGUISH YOUR BUSINESS AND CREATE OPPORTUNITIES

- *Shape your strategies and tactics so that they are not worn-out repetitions of yesterday's action.*

From the hard-earned lessons of past market campaigns and key events, sort out what worked, didn't work, and what could be salvaged for next-generation strategies.

Today's markets are in a state of flux. Small and large companies are reevaluating how they run their businesses; many are restructuring their organizations; others are realigning their work staffs.

In those voids are opportunities in once overlooked niches that could now open to you, or with services you can provide to a new customer group.

Specifically, for the smaller company, the primary advantage is its energy, flat organizational structure, and ability to shift gears rapidly. If your company doesn't fit that definition, it is a major opportunity to make changes.

- *Develop your strategies so they are balanced between two-zones of activity.*

Zone 1 seeks opportunities by focusing on customers' needs. If you expect to sustain growth and maintain a comfortable lead over hard-driving competitors, make certain customers as the center of your attention.

Zone 2 aims at preventing competitors from slowing down your efforts. In a flat-growth environment, they are doing all they can to outsell, outpromise, and outperform you to get the same customer. That is, they are ready to do whatever is necessary to take the business away from you. Therefore, focus your attention on devising strategies to make sure you are not blocked – and they do not succeed.

- *Align your business strategies with your organization's culture.*

This connection is often overlooked by managers. Yet, if you look for the intrinsic characteristics of your history, behavior, personality, you can find ways to make your company distinctive. Thus, the uniqueness of your firm's culture can distinguish your company and give it a definable advantage.

- *Maintain ongoing competitive intelligence.*

If you know your competitor's moves, you can determine with some accuracy which strategies will likely succeed and reject those with little chance of success.

Also, if you identify your rival's areas of vulnerability, you are in an ideal position to shape your product offerings, services, and marketing strategies, so that you apply your strengths against your competitor's weaknesses. (Review the uniqueness of applying an indirect strategy in Chapter 4.)

- *Lift employees' morale and encourage their trust.*

The intrepid leader is still the decisive ingredient in any venture. "When you're battling the marketplace, they need to know you will support them," declared a **3M Corp**. executive.

Key point:

The uniqueness of your firm's culture can distinguish your company and give it a definable advantage.

- *Instill discipline and training to prevent employees from caving-in against tough competitive situations.*

The intent is to avoid excessive caution that can result in loss of equilibrium, initiative, and a winning spirit. "People will take any hill, walk into the worst situation, if they have faith in their leadership and know what the strategies and objectives are," says a **Tyco International** senior manager.

- *Foster team solidarity that inspires innovation.*

For anything significant to happen, it is the mind and quality of the individual, as well as the unity of a team effort, that produces any meaningful effect. "You have to be open to diverse points of view. Given the speed of change, I don't know how a business will continue to flourish in the future without being receptive to different points of view," stated a **Tyco** executive.

From the above guidelines, we can now move forward and set functional rules you can follow to create opportunities, while holding off competitors' interferences.

RULES TO DISTINGUISH YOUR BUSINESS AND CREATE OPPORTUNITIES

Choose Boldness Over Excessive Caution

Most often, you can turn a risky competitive situation into a new opportunity by taking measured risks. Based on empirical evidence from a variety of disciplines, this principle points out that where individuals are stalled by lack of ideas and immobilized by fear severe problems can fester.

Apply Strength Against Weakness

The indirect approach is the indisputable principle, the one consistently successful component of a business strategy. It is the core element in creating opportunities.

By applying your weight against a competitor's weak points, you give yourself an edge. For instance, if you do a better job in solving customers' problems or in developing products and services, and you do so in a manner that your competitor is unable or unwilling to match, you gain a distinct advantage – even against the larger competitor. (The how-to is provided later in this chapter.)

> ***Key point:***
>
> The indirect approach is the one consistently successful component of a business strategy.

Use Speed to Secure a Competitive Lead

Rarely has an overlong, dragged-out campaign proved successful. Exhaustion through the draining of resources damages more companies than almost any other factor.

Further, speed doesn't mean running after every Monday-morning headline or expending resources in an impulsive and indiscriminate manner. It does mean that you have done your research, examined your options, assessed your people's skills, and reviewed the availability of other resources before moving forward.

Deploy, Target, Segment

Concentrate your resources so that you gain superiority in key segments that you select. Doing so places you in a position whereby you emerge stronger than your competitor. By integrating concentration into your business plans and strategies, you gain the distinct advantage of being able to compete successfully against a larger competitor. (See next chapter on segmentation.)

Use Competitive Intelligence as The Underpinnings of Your Business Strategy

Collect enough competitive intelligence to help you pinpoint the behavior of competing managers, as well as to assess their firm's physical strengths and weaknesses.

This rule connects with indirect strategy and concentration. The essential point: Without the input of competitive intelligence there is no reasonable way to implement an indirect or concentration strategy.

It is also worth repeating John D. Rockefeller's advice: "Next to knowing all about your own business, the best thing to know is all about the other fellow's business."

> ***Key point:***
>
> By integrating concentration into your business plans, you can compete successfully against a larger competitor.

Match Business Plans With Your Company Culture

Company culture is embedded as the nerve center of an organization. It guides how your employees think and react when entangled in a variety of hot spots.

A supportive corporate culture sets the tone and is the driver of forward-looking business decisions. It is the shaper of attitudes that generates customer loyalty and ignites employee involvement in seeking out opportunities.

"Stay focused on culture, people, and values. It's the area most likely to get compromised in this environment," declares a senior executive of **Pepsi Bottling Group**.

Leadership Skills Determine the Outcome of Your Expansion Plans

Leadership is about responsibility, accountability, and achieving corporate and business-unit objectives. Leaders inspire their people, organize actions, develop strategies, and respond to market and competitive uncertainty with speed and effectiveness.

Do all you can to hone your leadership skills so that they conform to your personal style, the nature of the people you are supervising, the types of short-and long-term objectives you are after, and the prevailing market conditions you face. That is all by way of saying, there is no one leadership style to fit all internal and external conditions.

As for the long-term: "If you don't invest in the future and don't plan for the future, there won't be one," says a key manager at 3M.

Create a Morale Advantage

Looking for opportunities also pertains to sensitive issues related to employee morale, discipline, and trust. And below that surface is an additional dimension: It is the human heart, the core of human emotion that reigns supreme during times of stress and tough competitive encounters. So that when all else fails, engage the hearts and emotions of your staff to go the extra mile.

Strengthen Your Decision-Making Capabilities

No event is a stand-alone occurrence. Therefore, study business history, look at past business events, and discover the roots of a problem. Doing so will help to fortify your intuition, enhance your business experience, and expand your overall knowledge. The result: You sharpen your decision-making and strategy skills.

Now, let's narrow the guidelines and rules even further with step-by-step applications in line with actual market conditions.

APPLICATIONS TO DISTINGUISH YOUR BUSINESS AND CREATE OPPORTUNITIES

More so than in past decades, companies, especially smaller ones, will face a mountain of challenges. The following list of actual problems represents concrete difficulties faced by executives. No doubt some are ones you are facing in one form or another at the present time[1]:

- How do we sustain growth in a sluggish market?
- With large organizations tending to dominate an industry, what strategies are possible?
- How can we identify long-term opportunities, yet manage day-to-day operations?
- How can we use competitor analysis to justify the time and expense of gathering the information?
- How do we deal with offshore competitors selling into our market with prices 30% to 40% below ours?
- How do we cope with the possibility of our product becoming a dinosaur?
- How can we solidify customer relationships to block enterprising competitors trying to make inroads against us?
- What defensive strategies are effective to protect our market share?
- How can we maneuver into a market already occupied by an industry leader?
- How can we justify the high upfront expenditures for new product development with the inevitable drop in prices as our products move rapidly into the mature stage of their life cycles?
- What strategies can help reverse a steep decline in our company's sales?
- As a smaller company, how can we apply customer-driven techniques to grow against dominant competitors?
- Is there a way to create a competitive advantage in a basic industry heavily dominated by large, low-cost competitors?

---

1. The list of problems comes from a survey of executives representing a variety of industries, which was conducted by a highly-regarded management publication.

- How do we make the culture of our organization the centerpiece of our strategy?
- How do we position our products effectively against the market leader?
- What strategies can outdistance competitors when entering a new market?
- What strategies can we use to regain lost market share?

Within the above framework of tangible problems, the following set of applications can apply to solving many of those problems – with potential relevance to your situation, as well:

1. Select an area that could represent a competitive advantage and which larger competitors cannot match.

Action: Table 6.1, Creating Problem-Solving Strategies, provides a comprehensive source for identifying strategies and opportunities.

Within each of the five columns are numerous opportunities. As you examine the items, make certain you do so within a framework of a two-zone strategy. That is, does the item you select represent a need for your customer; and does it surpass anything your competitor is likely to offer?

Also, give particular attention to the column, People. Here, you want to pinpoint areas in which you have a unique personnel advantage. The aim is to gain a competitive edge over your rivals. (You may wish to review Chapter 2 to see more detail about creating a people advantage.)

Table 6.1. Creating Problem-Solving Strategies

Product	Price	Communications	Supply Chain	People
Quality	List price	Advertising:	Channels:	Customer-driven attitude
Features	Discounts	Customer	Direct sales force	Positive vs. negative mindset
Options	Allowances	Trade	Distribution	Boldness vs. timidity
Style	Payment period		Dealers	Competitive spirit
Brand name	Credit terms	Personal selling:		Experience
Packaging		Incentives	Market coverage	Awareness
Sizes		Sales aids		Collective knowledge
Services		Samples	Warehouse	Skills
Warranties		Training	locations	Morale
Returns				Diversity
Versatility		Sales promotion:	Inventory control	Group unity
Uniqueness		Demonstrations	systems	Motivation
Utility		Contests		Endurance during tough times
Reliability		Premiums	Physical transport	
Durability		Coupons		Supportive company
Patent protection		Manuals		culture
Guarantees				Cooperative management
		Telemarketing		Work environment
		Internet		Internal communications
		Publicity		Planning capabilities
				Rewards system

2. Commit to quality and service as a company priority.

Action: Initiate programs that encourage individuals to strive for quality. Also, look for opportunities by focusing on the various stages of a product's sales life. (See Table 6.2.)

As shown in Table 6.2, different conditions characterize the stages of the product sales cycle. By monitoring the stages and then introducing appropriate strategies, you are in a better position to locate opportunities.

Table 6.2. Product Opportunities Throughout the Sales Cycle

Sales Cycle Stage	Product	Pricing	Supply Chain	Marketing
Introduction	Offer technically mature products, keep mix small	Use skim or high introductory pricing to price-insensitive innovators	Fill the pipeline to the consumer; distribute through intermediaries	Create primary demand for the product category; spend generously on promotion
Growth	Improve product; keep mix limited	Adjust price as needed to meet competition	Increase product presence and go for market penetration	Expand marketing effort to increase sales volume
Maturity	Distingish your product from competition; expand your product offering to satisfy different market segments	Capitalize on price-sensitive demand by further reducing prices	Take over wholesaling function (if feasible) by using a dedicated sales force	Differentiate your product in the minds of prospective buyers; emphasize brand appeal
Saturation	Proliferate your mix further, diversify into new markets	Keep prices stable	Intensify your distribution to increase availability and exposure	Support your market position
Decline	Prune your mix radically	Carefully increase prices	Consolidate your distribution setup; establish minimum orders	Reduce advertising activity to reminder level

STRATEGIES THROUGHOUT THE SALES CYCLE

Introduction

In this first stage, it is your task to create primary demand for your new product offering. Creating demand is an educational process that involves activating people's needs and focusing them on your product.

Initially, keep the product mix small to provide a clear focus and keep costs under control. Also, confine the mix to just a few variations that reflect the underlying concept of the entire category.

Try to lock your firm into long-term commitments to a selected group of middlemen. The degree to which you know how to secure maximum availability of your product in the right outlets can make or break your participation in the ongoing growth of a new market.

If you have a dedicated sales force and ongoing business relationships with prospects, you must sell them on the merits of your innovation. To this end, provide sufficient tangible incentives to motivate them to move ahead with speed.

Also essential is the support you give to your product in the form of advertising. Providing a new product with lukewarm advertising support is generally tantamount to dismal, if not failed, sales performance.

As for price, there are two choices: (1) choose penetration pricing, which aims at creating a mass market and discouraging competitive entry through low introductory prices; (2) consider a skim strategy that starts out with a comparatively high price and attempts to recover the initial outlays for product development and marketing, before competitive pressures erode your initial advantage.

Growth

In this second stage, you try to modify your basic product with value-added features and services, as well as solve any problems discovered through early consumer reactions. However, if the product is selling well, the product mix can remain small.

With the supply chain, your goal is to expand market coverage by signing up new channel members.

As for advertising, your emphasis is likely to shift from creating product awareness to expanding market volume. Also, prices soften as price-cutting competitors enter the market.

Maturity

The third stage turns into a fight for market share against other competitors. At this time, it pays to redesign your product to make it more distinctive and easier to differentiate from competitive offerings. It is also advisable to adopt a strategy of market segmentation to satisfy the unique needs of these fairly uniform groups within the market.

Look at your supply chain as it relates to effective market coverage, costs, and control. If you employed the services of wholesalers in your introductory thrust, think about shifting support to the primary ones that are pushing your product harder.

Your advertising has to communicate and enhance your drive to differentiate your product. It should emphasize brand appeal, so that the prospect recognizes and prefers your product even in a competitive environment. The effectiveness of your promotional efforts, however, is likely to decrease sharply as demand becomes less responsive to promotion because of growing brand loyalty, and resultant market resistance.

Since actual differences between substitute products are very slight and price sensitivity of demand is high, price variations between your firm's products and those of your competitors gain in importance. Prices will tend to drop further, but stabilize toward the end of the stage as a result of cost pressures.

Saturation

As your product enters the next stage of its sales cycle, typically a no-holds-barred fight develops for market share. Because market volume has ceased to improve, the growth of your sales volume is achieved at the expense of competitors.

In your product strategy, attempt to differentiate your offering by adding value choices. Because of the limited growth potential, it will pay to pursue a strategy of diversification. For instance, it might be worth moving into other geographic markets where your product could be at the introduction or growth stages of a new sales cycle.

Your channel strategy remains unaltered in the saturation phase. You should attempt to gain even more intensive distribution and, thereby, maximize availability and exposure.

Your advertising strategy at this point is to maintain the status quo. Little new ground can be broken, so advertising of the reminder or reinforcement type is needed.

Decline

With consumer interest on the decline, competitors drop out of the market in droves. If you are still in the market, you will trim your product offerings, vigorously weed out weak products, and concentrate on a few profitable ones.

Similarly, you will attempt to reduce distribution cost, such as establishing minimum orders to discourage small shipments.

Your sales effort will tend to be low key, with emphasis on retaining as much of your market as you can. Advertising support will diminish to the low-budget, infrequent-reminder type. Your prices will stay right about where they are.

3. Focus on specialty products that command premium prices. Leave the commodity price segment to others, unless you are the low-cost producer.

Action: Practice marketing your product with specific applications, which forces you to get closer to your customers and their problems.

For instance, look at the following possibilities for your products:

- Promote more frequent usage of your product among existing customers.
- Find new users for your product.
- Find more uses (applications) for your product.
- Find new uses for your product's basic materials.

4. Establish long-term interactions with customers by building technology and product relationships.

Action: Encourage trust with customers so that sensitive information can be shared for mutual interests. If possible, utilize them to design product features, propose product options, or identify new services.

New product opportunities come in many different forms. This diversity can span the range from technological innovation to market newness, or just cosmetic changes.

For technological change, look to modification, line extension, and diversification. For market newness, differentiate between remerchandising and market extension.

With any changes you anticipate, be aware that from a consumer and marketing perspective, a new product is viewed as new when it is perceived in the marketplace as new.

Table 6.3 presents the differences among five categories of new products and points out the benefits of each.

Table 6.3. New Product Opportunities

Category	Definition	Nature	Benefit
Modification	Alter a product feature	Same number of product lines and products	Combines the new with the familiar
Line extension	Add more variety	Same number of product lines, higher number of products	Segments the market by offering more choice
Diversification	Enter a new business	New product line, higher number of products	Spreads the risk and capitalizes on opportunities
Remerchandising	Market change to create a new impression	Same products, same markets	Generates excitement and stimulates sales
Market extension	Enter a new market	Same products, new market	Broadens the base

Key point:

Utilize customer input to design product features, propose product options, or identify new services.

Rarely will the five new product categories be used separately. They lend themselves to combined applications for maximum impact. Moreover, you will probably want to try a package approach to maintain steady growth.

For instance, line extension is often used with remerchandising or market extension. Diversification is often combined with market extension. The use of one category does not preclude the application of other approaches at the same time, possibly within the same market. What remains essential, though, is that the prospective customer perceives a difference worthy of consideration.

5. Maintain a market-driven orientation throughout your organization.

Action: Organize a strategy team made up of individuals that represent a variety of functions. Then use the team's business plan as a guide to market opportunities. (Strategic business planning is discussed in Chapter 8 and a strategy team's duties and responsibilities are listed in Chapter 2, Table 2.3.)

6. Investigate opportunities that complement your long-term objectives.

Action: Seek joint ventures, licensing, or exporting situations that can expand your presence in existing markets, as well as secure a foothold in developing markets.

7. Partner salespeople with customers to provide product solutions to customers' problems.

Action: Go beyond traditional forms of sales training. Instead, teach salespeople how to think like strategists, so they can help their customers achieve a competitive advantage.

Also, consider offering training as a value-added service to your customers using online or live workshops. Table 6.4, How to Think Like a Strategist, provides a format for training both your personnel and for customer use[2].

Table 6.4. Workshop Outline: How to Think Like a Strategist

Key Topics	Discussion Points and Activities
Search for opportunities in unserved, poorly served, or emerging market segments.	Penetrate new and expand existing market segments. Improve products and services. Stretch product lines. Position product to the needs of customers and against competitors.

2. For use as a workshop, this outline would be expanded with the content from selected chapters of this book and linked to specific information from your company.

Identify ways to create new opportunities.	Participate in current technologies, initiate product and service innovations, explore new delivery systems. Pioneer something new or unique.
Look for opportunities through marketing creativity.	Promote image, quality, performance, training. Explore fresh approaches in Internet marketing, social networking, and other online activities.
Monitor customer relationships and retention rates.	Discover dominant reasons for strong customer relationships. Identify reasons why customers leave: - measure retention rate - isolate causes of customer defections - calculate lost profits - determine types of value-added services and differentiation approaches to retain customers.
Monitor changing buying behavior.	Practice segmenting markets according to changing behavioral patterns. Identify clusters of customers who might buy or utilize different services for different reasons.
Learn from competitors – and adapt strategies from other industries.	Understand competitors: - how they conduct business - what products they sell - what strategies they pursue - how they manufacture, distribute, and price - what weaknesses, limitations, and vulnerabilities they exhibit.
Use strategy to create and maintain a competitive advantage.	Create differentiation in such areas as: Quality, function, service, warranties, applications. (See Table 6.1.)
Utilize entrepreneurial thinking by challenging the status quo.	Recognize that continuous incremental changes can often beat occasional revolutionary breakthroughs. Look for ways to: - introduce new products - modify existing products - alter perception of products or services in customers' minds - pursue new customers and increase product usage by existing customers.

Identify distinctive competencies and turn them into competitive advantages.	Highlight and exploit such areas as: - special skills unique to your firm - marketing abilities - customer/dealer relationships - product innovations - ability to build market position and retain customer loyalty - capability to confront competition without hesitating.
Recognize that minor or emerging competitors can hurt you more than highly visible competitors.	Maintain a comprehensive market and competitor intelligence system that focuses on customers and competitors built around a two-zone strategy.
Understand that timing is as important as strategy choice.	Use speed. Maintain movement when competitor is unable or unwilling to respond. Time actions most conducive to dealer support and customer response. Use strategy to unbalance competitors into making wrong moves.
Creating opportunities are conditional on quality of personnel, company culture, and market factors.	Uphold a customer-driven company culture. Work closely with the staff in creating opportunities. Pay close attention to the psychological dimension of your people, identified by: attitude, morale, state of mind, overall way of thinking.
Strategy development and implementation are outcomes of strategic business plans.	Seek opportunities within your area of responsibility. Look to competitive advantage as an object of strategy. Search for and exploit distinctive competencies unique to your company. Avoid complacency, reexamine all assumptions, objectives, and strategies used in business plans.

Key point:

Teach salespeople how to think like strategists.

8. Monitor your company's and product's image.

Action: An image evolves from a multitude of factors. It can include the choice of a company or brand name, the symbolism used, or any other part of the entire marketing spectrum, including product design, pricing, and promotion. The symbolism also contains logos, slogans, jingles, colors, shapes, or packaging.

If you want to strategically shape your product's image, Table 6.5 offers useful guidelines. You will find numerous image ingredients that are under your control, along with highlights of their respective roles in determining an overall image. Be sure, however, that the image is consistent with your long-term business plan.

Table 6.5. Shaping Your Company's and Product's Image

Controllable Image Ingredients	What They Can Do
Design	Provides esthetic appeal
Color	Sets a mood
Shape	Generates recognizability
Package	Connotes value and function
Name	Expresses central idea
Slogan, jingle, logo	Creates memorability
Advertising, personal selling	Communicates benefits
Sales promotion	Stimulates interest
Price	Suggests quality, value, prestige
Warranty	Establishes believability
Service	Substantiates product support

9. Identify market niches that are emerging, neglected, or poorly served.

Action: Reassess how you segment your markets. Search for additional approaches beyond the usual criteria of customer size, frequency of purchase, and geographic location. Look for potential niches related to just-in-time delivery, performance, application, quality, or technical assistance. (See Chapter 7.)

Once again, use Figure 6.1 to select a strategy area that builds a unique competitive advantage for your company or product line.

10. Use information technology to link customers, suppliers, business partners, and employees.

    Action: Encourage a continuous flow of information by engaging in ongoing communications from product concept to delivery of a product to a customer. Effectively applied, informational technology performs as a powerful competitive strategy and an effective link that allows you to be more virtual with customers and suppliers.

11. Search for acquisitions, marketing relationships, and other forms of partnering as keys to success.

    Action: To make alliances work requires a high level of trust and willingness to achieve mutually agreed-upon, short- and long-term goals.

    That means that your company's culture – expressed as values, ideas, and behavioral patterns – has to be compatible with the culture of the other firm in the alliance, if you expect the relationship to succeed in forming healthy interactions with customers, suppliers, and employees.

    Specifically, success relies on understanding your company's core values, maintaining a positive mindset, and an orientation that is totally customer-driven.

> ***Key point:***
>
> Continuous incremental changes can often beat occasional revolutionary breakthroughs.

Summarizing: This chapter delivers a set of guidelines, rules, and applications that prepares you to think like a strategist, with particular attention to creating opportunities.

How, then, does the total process play-out in a real world market situation? Let's look at one industry, food, where generics were biting into sales of branded products, where consumer tastes were changing, and in general sales were flat.

Food companies representing branded products saw opportunities in such a marketplace by latching on to the popular food trend for better nutrition and taste. Several companies in the industry responded by packing more of their products with high amounts of fiber.

Examples include:

Danone SA's Activia using new food technology to overcome consumers' traditional distaste for some items introduced a line of yogurt containing an additional three grams of fiber for better taste and healthier nutrition.

Kellogg Co. realigned the bulk of its U.S. cereals by modifying its content to contain at least 10% more fiber.

General Mills Inc. developed line extensions by expanding its Fiber One line of cereals to include snack bars, baking mixes, and yogurts. They also rolled out a new line of Progresso soups with 28% of recommended daily fiber intake per cup.

While the above examples focus on the consumer, one issue is not covered: *competition*. If you look again at the two-zone strategy discussed earlier, then you see that the above action points only on zone one: the *consumer*.

As for zone two – preventing competition from unrailing the consumer-directed strategy – this issue did not escape the branded product managers' attention. The above food companies expected to fend-off attacks by lower-priced private label products by adding fiber, which tends to be costly. "It will be extremely difficult for private labels to copy," declared a senior executive at Kellogg.

Applications: In the above brief examples, food companies faced problems of flat-growth, intensified competition, and changing consumer behavior. The following points illustrate the key parts of the opportunity-creating process covered in this chapter. They are ones you can employ – regardless of your industry or size of your company – to create opportunities.

For instance, consider the following sampling of guidelines, rules, and applications:

1. Food company managers maintained ongoing competitive and market intelligence to track market trends, consumer

tastes, and buying behavior. They also considered vulnerabilities of the private-label producers and their attachment to being low-cost, low-price providers.

2. Managers used segmentation techniques to identify those customer groups concerned with nutrition and taste. Then, they modified their product lines by adding fiber to their respective products. In effect those managers targeted an emerging market niche and moved in with speed.
3. Managers focused on specialty products that in many instances commanded premium prices, thereby improving their ability to maintain profitability levels. Doing so, also set up private label competitors to be reactive by placing them in an uncomfortable position that could disrupt their low-price strategy.
4. Managers (consciously or not) addressed the two-zone strategy by looking both at consumers and competitors.

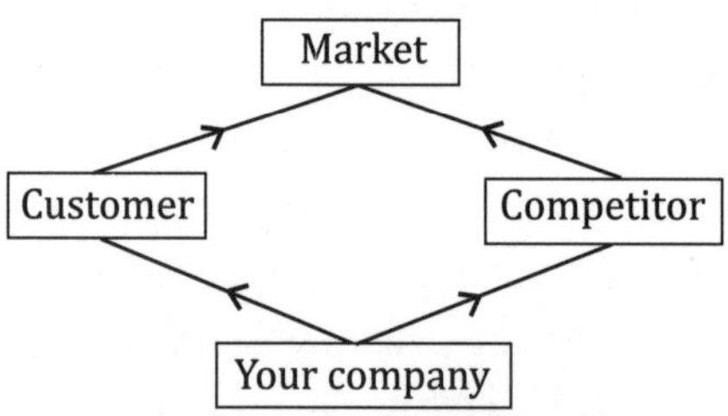

Figure 6.1. Two-Zone Strategy

5. They devised strategies to extend the sales life of their products, thereby avoiding the saturation and decline stages by using, in part, new food technologies.
6. Underlying the opportunity-development process is people. It is through a staff that is motivated with above-average attitudes, morale, and mindsets that assures success. All of which, in turn, aligns with each company's culture.

Now, let's move on to Chapter 7, 'Segment Your Markets', which is another term for implementing a strategy of concentration.

7

Segment Your Markets

What does a segmented market look like? How would you identify opportunities?

Let's look at segments from a variety of viewpoints:

First, from a broad perspective, China is an outstanding case in point that gives credibility to the power of concentrating your resources.

With its enormous population of 1.3 billion, speaking more than 100 dialects, China is about as diversified as any single country can be from a marketing perspective. And it is in its diversity that segmentation plays a central role in developing a viable portfolio of opportunities. What people eat, wear, and drive differs greatly from north to south, east to west, rich to poor, young to old, city to countryside.

From a manager's position, China is a superb example of the potential opportunities when using concentration to penetrate a market. Succeeding with concentration, however, incorporates a three-step process:

- Employ market intelligence to define customer segments and evaluate competitors.
- Pinpoint a segment for initial entry; once secured, then systematically roll-out into additional market segments.
- Customize products to those segments.

Second, let's examine a specific application when entering a new market and introducing an innovative product where the company had no prior experience in the targeted marketplace and the company's name and product was unknown.

That was the situation with Chinese automaker **BYD Co.** when it finalized plans for an all-electric battery car that takes about seven to nine hours to fully charge when plugged into a regular home outlet. The business plan called for building its brand name in North America by offering one model, a five-seat car, before eventually expanding its offerings.

The launch strategy pinpointed a specific segment within the U.S. with a projected initial sale of a few hundred units through a small number of dealers and priced at slightly more than $40,000. Defining the segment more precisely, one BYD executive stated, "In the beginning, out target customers are going to be government agencies, utilities, and some celebrities."

Third, there is still another perspective that illustrates ways to create opportunities through segmentation, which has special application for smaller firms. The segment involves an overlooked group:

For a long period of time marketers generally avoided the boomer generation – people born between 1946 and 1964. They assumed that the boomers' behavioral patterns and brand choices were hardened and that their biggest earning and spending years were behind them.

Those assumptions proved wrong on all counts. Once awakened to the reality that a large and vacant segment was up for grabs, the more savvy managers began reexamining the boomers and came up with startling discoveries: Strong evidence revealed that this ignored group is far from sluggish, inactive, and set in their ways.

Instead, with average life expectancy at an all-time high in many developed countries, individuals over age 50 consider the middle age years as a new start in life and act as if they will be around for two or three decades.

Surveys further indicated that few boomers planned to stop work altogether as they age. With children grown and out of the house, the lifestyles shaped up like this: Second careers start, boomers strive to stay mentally and physically active, and they are open to new experiences and products.

Those signals awakened some companies to move rapidly and gain a solid foothold in a previously disregarded segment that now exhibits outstanding promise for long-term growth. The promise is great, however, for managers with the know-how and focused strategy to make opportunity a reality.

Yet, within that rosy picture, there is still a lesson to be noted: Even with a potentially huge market destined to keep growing, the worst strategy is to attack the entire market. Instead, the concentration rule emphatically states:

Go into segments with products and services where you have unique and definable strengths. Otherwise, you squander budgeted resources and chase after niches that entail unnecessary risks.

In particular, for the smaller company, your best course of action is to focus on selected market segments where you enjoy a measurable and substantial advantage over competitors. Advantage in this framework translates to creating strategies built around product differentiation, value-added services, and business solutions that exceed those offered by your competitors.

The above examples illustrate that employing segmentation means splitting the overall market into smaller submarkets or niches and then concentrating your resources. Doing so gives you a significant chance to win over a larger competitor that may be spreading resources over numerous segments and can only allocate a modest expenditure to your segment.

Also, subdividing the market helps you identify and satisfy the specific needs of selected groups, thereby helping to strengthen your market position. Thus, segmentation allows you to concentrate your strength against the weaknesses of your competitors, at which point you can improve your competitive ranking.

Are there any negatives to segmentation? Why should you concentrate all your resources at a customer group, geographic segment, or a single competitor? Aren't you placing all your resource eggs in one precarious basket and taking on undue risk?

Also, what impact would such a strategy have on how your firm is organized? For instance, do you centralize the sales force or technical staff to handle all customers and products, or do you divide them according to customer segments and product lines?

The hardnosed evidence leads unequivocally to adopting a strategy that aims at concentrating resources where you can gain superiority in as few areas as possible. Consider the following guidelines:

> ***Key point:***
>
> Segmenting the market helps you identify and satisfy the specific needs of individuals and thereby strengthens your competitive position.

SEGMENTATION GUIDELINES

1. You can't be all things to all people. Even huge, global organizations will shy away from pursuing such a generally fruitless effort, unless they have sufficient resources to be a segment leader in all markets, which is not the typical case for the smaller organization.
2. Where there is an overwhelming leader in the market, your best strategy is to concentrate your strength and strike one point that represents your competitor's weakness.
3. Your best course of action is to acquire market intelligence that documents the specific needs and problems of a well-defined customer group and then concentrate your resources.
4. Look for a customer segment that represents a market trend, or find a niche that has been overlooked, neglected, or poorly served.

There is one additional benefit to segmentation: You have a greater ability to latch on to relationship marketing. This means building long-term satisfying relations with key parties – customers, suppliers, distributors – in order to retain their long-term preference and business. The intent is to deliver high quality, distinctive service, at competitive prices to customers.

Relationships can run the gamut from an almost nonexistent one of a salesperson simply selling a product to that of a flourishing relationship where partnering means working consistently with a customer to discover ways to generate customer savings.

Or it can mean helping the customer design a product for its customers. In some instances relationships can include placing an individual on the customer's premises to assist in a variety of tasks from inventory control to providing technical assistance.

Thus, the movement is well on its way from transaction marketing to relationship marketing. To implement the transition, your approach is to track customers and determine which ones are worthy of the full services of relationship marketing. Therefore,

- Identify the key customers warranting relationship marketing.
- Train the salesperson or other contact individual to deal exclusively with the customer.
- Require a customer-relationship plan that details the objectives, actions, and required resources to implement the program.
- Make the Internet and related technology an integral part of the customer relationship plan.

IDENTIFYING A MARKET SEGMENT

Your ability to accurately concentrate resources in a segment that will yield the greatest payout over the long-term is a skill you need to exploit. For instance, you should know which criteria to use in choosing market segments and how to develop a segmentation analysis.

Use the following criteria to guide you in selecting market segments:

- *Measurable.* Can you quantify the segment? For example, you should be able to quantify how many factories, how many engineers, or how many people with or without access to technical service exist within the market segment.
- *Accessible.* Do you have access to the market through a dedicated sales force, distributors/dealers, transportation, or the Internet?
- *Substantial.* Is the segment of adequate size to warrant your attention as a viable segment? Further, is the segment declining, maturing, or growing?
- *Profitable.* Does concentrating on the segment provide sufficient profitability to make it worthwhile? Use your organization's standard measurements for profitability, such as return on investment, gross margin, or profits.
- *Compatible with Competition.* To what extent do your major competitors have an interest in the segment? Is it of active interest or of negligible concern to your competitors?
- *Effectiveness.* Do your people have acceptable skills and resources to serve the segment effectively?
- *Defendable.* Does your firm have the capabilities to defend itself against the attack of a major competitor?

Key point:

You can identify market segments by dividing a market into groups of customers with common characteristics.

Answering those questions will help you decide on a market segment with good potential for concentrating your resources, as well as for gaining ample information about your customers and competitors. Once selected, the above criteria can be used to test the feasibility of a market segment. (While computer software may speed up the segmentation process, be certain the above criteria are included when you select the program.)

CLASSIC TECHNIQUES TO SELECTING A MARKET SEGMENT

Table 7.1 displays the four most common ways to segment a market, based on demographic, geographic, psychographic, and product attribute factors. Each of these approaches can be subdivided into additional niches. Or they can be used in various combinations to create fresh opportunities. Let's examine each:

Table 7.1. Bases for Market Segmentation

Demographic Segmentation	Psychographic Segmentation
Sex Age Family life cycle Race/ethnic group Education Income Occupation Family size Religion Home ownership	Lifestyles Psychological variables: - Personality - Self-image - Cultural influences
Geographic Segmentation	**Product Attribute Segmentation**
Region Urban/suburban/rural Population density City size Climate	Usage rate Product benefits

> ***Key point:***
>
> Demographics are easier to observe and measure than most other characteristics.

Demographic Segmentation

Demographic variables are among the most widely used segmentation approaches. They owe their popularity to two facts:

First, they are easier to observe and/or measure than most other characteristics.

Second, their breakdown of sex, age, family life cycle, race/ ethnic group, education, income, occupation family size, religion, and home ownership are often closely linked to differences in behavioral patterns.

In many instances, you can combine demographic variables to produce a more meaningful breakdown than just relying on a single criterion. For example, it is common to combine the age of the head of the household with the family size and the level of household income.

If four age levels, three family sizes, and three income levels are distinguished, a total of 36 segments result. Using a combination of primary data, secondary data, and judgment, you can then determine the value of each segment and thus arrive at a well-thought-out conclusion about the segments that warrant your efforts.

Watch out, however, for unrelated demographic characteristics that could be unreliable: Gender may produce marginal differences in the usage patterns of telephones or in the consumption of toothpaste and soft drinks. Or chronological age is not always a reliable indicator of behavioral patterns and income level may prove relevant only when used with other variables such as social class, family life cycle, and occupation.

Geographic Segmentation

Geographic segmentation is relatively easy to perform because the individual segments can be clearly defined on a map. It is a sensible strategy to employ when there are distinct differences in climatic conditions, access to transportation, proximity to round-the-clock service or repairs – as well as with such geographic considerations as varying regional tastes or unique culture-based habits and behaviors.

Geographic segmentation even extends to facial features used in advertising. When **Kodak** originally introduced its Instamatic camera worldwide, the company quickly learned through adverse market feedback that potential consumers in many countries around the globe, from the Philippines to India, from Hong Kong to South Africa, could not relate to the Caucasian girl portrayed in the advertising. Kodak promptly modified its advertising by using local models that contributed to a phenomenal success story.

Internationally, blocks or clusters of countries can often be approached in a similar fashion, particularly if they share the same language and cultural heritage. For instance, in Latin America the same advertising media are often appropriate for several countries.

While there are numerous cultural differences in many of those countries there are common problems with shared features, known as cultural universals. These include economic issues, marriage and family rituals, educational systems, religious observance, and supernatural beliefs.

Geographically, you can segment by region, city size, by population density, or by other geopolitical criteria. However, such segmentation is effective only if it reflects differences in need and buying patterns. Some entrepreneurs, for example, can adjust their advertising efforts to target very narrowly defined groups.

For instance, **Panera Bread Co.**, a restaurant chain, has maintained prices and in some cases increased them even during a recession-wracked economy. Its management bucked conventional industry wisdom by avoiding discounts. Instead, they targeted customers who can still spend an average of about $8.50 for lunch, where other chains offered meals for as little as $5.

Further, Panera has been able to persuade customers to pay premiums because it has been improving the quality of its food.

"Most of the world seems to be focused on a segment of the population who are unemployed. We've focused on the 90% that are still employed," stated a senior Panera executive.

> ***Key point:***
>
> Even where numerous cultural differences exist, there are common problems that share common features, known as cultural universals.

Psychographic Segmentation

This form of segmentation results from the application of psychographic variables, such as lifestyle, personality, and self-image. Banks, food manufacturers, liquor producers, and restaurants, such as Panera, to name a few, benefit from the advantages of psychographic segmentation.

If you are astute enough you can observe the behavioral nuances of distinct target groups. Otherwise, you may need the professional help of individuals trained in some aspects of the social sciences.

For instance, you might watch how some groups that fit your customer profile live, spend, and behave. You can explore the activities they get involved with, interests they pursue, and opinions they hold.

Some individuals who may be disadvantaged tend to be depressed, withdrawn, and struggling to get out of poverty. Others may be more upbeat.

Still others might be ambitious, upwardly mobile, and status conscious. Not far behind are the individuals who are pursuing a rich inner life and want to experience directly what life has to offer.

The intent here is to open your thinking to the variety of ways to look at customer groups, so that you can develop alternate approaches to segmenting a market. Therefore, it is possible for you to use a form of lifestyle segmentation by observing the behavior of distinct target groups.

Product Attributes

Product attributes include usage rates defined as: nonuser, ex-user, potential user, first-time user, and regular user groups.

In practice, such information is further broken down to distinguish nonusers as light, medium, and heavy users of the product. Often, heavy users of a product represent a relatively small share of total households or corporate buyers, yet account for the major portion of the sales volume in the market.

These breakdowns, in turn, would trigger different motivational appeals to improve the level of responsiveness from various segments. In other applications, companies with high market share might be especially eager to attract potential users, while smaller competitors with lower market share would devote its efforts to converting existing users.

Overall, you will find product attributes most practical in segmenting a market, and particularly applicable in deciding where to deploy a sales force, allocate budgets, prioritize product development projects, and direct promotional campaigns for maximum impact.

The following case illustrates several of the points made thus far:

A small stationery company produced a basic, undistinguishable product line consisting of notebooks and two-pocket portfolios in a variety of colors. It fell victim to off-shore, low-priced competitors from China, Brazil, and Indonesia.

Adding to the predicament, the company's personnel suffered from an inbred company culture, characterized as an inside-out, rather than an outside-in orientation. Meaning: If its machines couldn't make it, the company didn't sell it.

The issue, then: Change or die. Rather than let the company go under, management took a proactive approach and looked hard at its market with the aim of getting inside the heads of customers and prospects and reacting to their needs and wants.

Initially, they looked at the teen market and defined that segment by fashion, color, design, and personality. Designers saw the ordinary notebook as really a medium for highly personal reflections and self-expression. The once drab notebook evolved into a fashion product. The commodity, inexpensive notebook became history.

Along with the product-line change came a transformation in the mindset of those running the company. Demographic and life style issues took center stage as the primary criteria defining market segments and product development.

Then, notwithstanding a meager budget, management invested in market research, something almost unknown in its history. In addition to buying consumer studies and assembling its first focus groups, the company began sending individuals on trend-spotting trips. By combining quantitative research along with qualitative observation, the company moved from a money-losing operation to a mover and shaker in its field.

ADVANCED TECHNIQUES TO SELECTING A MARKET SEGMENT

Beyond the more conventional techniques listed above, there is an advanced procedure that uses a strategy-driven approach to selecting a market segment.

The technique consists of classifying markets as: *natural, leading edge, key, linked, central, challenging, difficult*, and *encircled*.

Using these eight categories as a guide, you can look with a more critical eye at what challenges you will face. Then, you will be better able to assess the risks and potential rewards when selecting your strategies.

As you examine the characteristics for each market category, you may find some overlapping. That is acceptable since there are inherent commonalities among the various markets.

Natural Markets

In this type of marketplace, you operate in the familiar setting of your established markets. The implication is that within such customary surroundings, personnel tend to be at ease and may not be motivated to venture out of their comfort zone.

Yet, to expand, you have to motivate them to move beyond the confines of existing markets. That means you should get back to the issue of your organization's culture. That is, does your organization's culture permit venturing out of familiar territory?

For the most part, in a natural market, you and your rivals have learned to adopt a live-and-let-live policy. That condition exists as long as each company sticks to its own dedicated segment. Generally, outright aggressive confrontations are seldom used.

The primary reason for this uncharacteristic display of togetherness in a highly competitive world is that you and your rivals share a common interest in furthering the long-term growth and prosperity of the market.

On the other hand, if any one competitor chooses to move forward and gain a meaningful benefit, a likely strategy might include securing a more advantageous position on the supply chain by adjusting its position. Or it can be done by adding or deleting a link in the distribution network. Or it may choose to gain additional market share by recasting itself as a low-cost producer.

Notwithstanding, even with the mayhem of global rivals scrambling for market share, or price wars eating away at profitability, it is still possible to have some semblance of market unity in natural markets.

There is one additional dimension that characterizes this category, which you should actively keep in the forefront of your thinking: Industries, markets, and products go through successive life cycle stages from introduction, growth, maturity, decline, to phase-out.

Much of the movement through those stages is driven by the adoption rate of technology, which precedes or follows changes in consumer behavior. There are also external changes triggered by legislative or environmental factors, generally out of a manager's ability to control.

To maintain growth, take the lead in the search for new segments in which to concentrate. Then, you can provide the momentum that drives new product development.

> ***Key point:***
>
> Industries, markets, and products go through life cycle stages from introduction, growth, maturity, decline, to phase-out.

Leading Edge Markets

Leading edge means exploring markets by making minor penetrations into a competitor's territory. The intent is to investigate the possibility of opening another revenue stream.

Therefore, you want to acquire the following types of intelligence:

- The feasibility of the market to generate a revenue stream over the long-term; and the possibility to expand into additional niches.
- The amount of investment needed to enter and gain a foothold in the market.
- A timeframe for payback and eventual profitability.
- An assessment of competitors: their market position, strengths/weaknesses, and nature of the opposition you will likely face.

A classic example of a leading edge market is the initial penetration by a few Japanese companies into the North American market with small copier machines. **Xerox**, the market leader in those early years, concentrated its marketing efforts at large corporations with a line of large copiers.

Xerox managers initially avoided the small copier market. That oversight proved to be a critical error. Armed with a low-cost, no-frills desktop copier, enterprising Japanese copier makers moved in virtually unopposed and exploited a wide-open opportunity in the vast market of small- and mid-size firms. Once established, they moved upscale in a segment-by-segment assault and took over a significant amount of Xerox's primary market share.

Key Markets

Key means that you and many of your competitors seem evenly matched within key market segments. The general behavior is that you would not openly oppose an equally strong rival.

However, you may find that a competitor is attempting to dislodge you from a long-held position with the clear aim of taking away customers or disrupting your supply chain relationships. Then you may be forced to launch a counter-effort by concentrating as many resources as possible to blunt the effort. Such actions are appropriate, however, if they fit your overall strategic objectives.

Therefore, keep the big picture in mind: If you expend excessive resources in hawkish-style actions such as price wars, then you may be left with a restricted budget to defend your market position. Therefore, use indirect strategies discussed in Chapter 4.

Linked Markets

In this category, you and your competitors are linked with easy access to markets. Your best strategy is to pay strict attention to constructing barriers around those niches that you value most, and from which you can best defend your position.

Barriers include:

- Above-average quality
- Feature-loaded products
- First-class customer service
- Superior technical support

- Competitive pricing
- On-time delivery
- Generous warranties
- Patent protection

Not only do you build barriers against competitors' incursions, you also benefit by solidifying customer relationships. In particular, customer loyalty gives you a long-lasting, profit-generating advantage that is difficult for a competitor to overcome. It is the one area that makes a meaningful addition to your growth. As one management analyst put it:

"If you currently retain 70 percent of your customers and you start a program to improve that to 80 percent, you'll add an additional 10 percent to your growth rate."

Key point:

Customer loyalty gives you a long-lasting, profit-generating advantage that is difficult for a competitor to overcome.

Central Markets

Central means that you may face powerful forces that threaten your market position. These forces are as diverse as watching competitors eat away at your position through aggressive pricing, or by offering dazzling feature-laden products, or by technology-rich firms generating new applications overlaid with value-added services.

To counter such threats, look for joint ventures so that the cumulative effects yield greater market advantages and offer more strategy options than you can achieve independently. For many companies the merger and acquisition (M&A) route and other forms of joint ventures have proven the strategy of choice.

Challenging Markets

In this category, if you enter a market dominated by a strong and aggressive competitor, be watchful. You could place your company at excessively high risk.

If, however, your long-term objectives strongly support maintaining a presence in a challenging market, and if the expenditures of financial, material, and human resources are consistent with your overall strategy, then find a secure position, for example, on the supply chain.

It could be one of your single best chances for lessening the risk and achieving a solid measure of success. Your aim is to rely on efficient distribution to ensure the movement of finished products to customers.

Dell Computer is a prime example of excellent supply chain management. The company activated its manufacturing process and the supply chain only when an order was received from a customer. That strategy eliminated the cost of storing excessive inventory.

Dell benefited by shipping just the right amount of components to its factories, thereby avoiding investing in expensive warehousing. For instance, in one facility, what used to be done in more than two buildings now is accomplished in one by applying the techniques of supply chain management.

Difficult Markets

This type of market segment is characterized as one where progress is erratic and highly competitive. If attempting to make any meaningful market penetration, secure key accounts, or maintain reasonable levels of logistical support, you are likely to be blocked by asset-draining barriers.

Also, if a competitor is fully prepared, takes you off-guard, and you subsequently lose your market position, it is difficult to return to your former position. In effect, you are entrapped in an untenable condition and your entire business strategy could be in jeopardy.

Your best course of action is to go forward, just as long as the effort is consistent with your mission and long-term strategic objectives.

Encircled Markets

Encircled segments foretell a potentially risky situation. This market condition exists where you control limited resources and any aggressive action by a stronger, well-positioned competitor can force you to consider pulling out of a market.

Therefore, it is in your best interest to maintain ongoing competitive intelligence, so that you can accurately assess the vulnerability of your position against that of your opponent.

Armed with the intelligence, you are able to develop a contingency plan that highlights your strengths and exposes your competitor's weaknesses. If in your judgment you still lack maneuverability and a capability to mount a meaningful competitive response, then exiting the market is prudent, as long as it minimizes disruption to your main line of business.

If, on the other hand, your competitor foresees an untenable position, it is wise to give the rival a way out of the market and not force him into a fight-to-the-end mindset.

Strategies include: (a) exploit a competitor's weaknesses and aggressively stay ahead by developing product enhancements, (b) launch value-added services, and (c) initiate any other programs that would hamper his ability to maintain a profitable market position.

The aim of these strategies is to discourage your opponent from making a monumental effort to fight you. Instead, encourage him to take the more tempting approach and exit the market. To implement the three-part strategy, it is best to form cross-functional teams. Table 7.2 summarizes the eight categories of market segments.

Key point:

Maintain ongoing competitive intelligence to accurately assess the vulnerability of your position against that of your opponent.

Table 7.2. Advanced Techniques for Market Segmentation

Category	Characteristics
Natural Market	You and your rivals can operate harmoniously as long as each company sticks to its own dedicated segment. Aggressive confrontations are seldom used. All companies share a common interest in furthering the long-term growth and prosperity of the market.
Leading Edge Market	Market entry means a minor penetration into a competitor's territory to determine the feasibility for generating a long-term revenue stream.
Key Market	Competitors appear evenly matched within key market segments. The general strategy is that you would not openly oppose an equally strong rival. If the competitor attacks your position, then you are forced to launch a counter-effort by concentrating as many resources to blunt the competitor's attack.
Linked Market	You and your competitors are linked with easy access to markets. Your best strategy is to construct barriers around those niches that you value most, and from which you can best defend your position.
Central Market	You face powerful competitors that threaten your market position. Counter such threats by joint venturing with firms so that you gain greater market advantages and develop additional strategy options than you would be able to accomplish independently.
Challenging Market	An aggressive competitor dominates the market and thereby could place your company at excessively high risk. However, if your long-term objectives strongly support maintaining a presence in the market, then one prudent approach is to secure a solid position on the supply chain.
Difficult Market	Competition is pervasive and market behavior is erratic. Gaining and maintaining market penetration is difficult. Overall, your best course of action is to go forward only if the effort is consistent with the objectives of your overall business plan.

Encircled Market	This market is risky where any aggressive action by a stronger, well-positioned competitor can force you out of the market. Maintain ongoing competitive intelligence to accurately assess the vulnerability of your position against that of your opponent. If you lack a capability to mount a meaningful competitive response, then exiting the market is a prudent strategy.

Recapping: Familiarizing yourself with the eight categories of markets will equip you with additional insights when selecting segments to enter and strategies to pursue.

Further, if you are able to concentrate your resources, rather than create an unequal distribution that dissipates your strength, you are in an excellent position to successfully exploit your opponent's weaknesses.

By that means, you conserve resources for unexpected opportunities that would otherwise be denied to you. It also permits you to defend against an unforeseen attack from a competitor. Such thinking and positioning are marks of an effective manager.

In order to make the most of concentration in your business strategy, use the following guidelines:

- Use competitive analysis to identify your competitors' weaknesses or market gaps. Doing so gives you the opportunity to shape your competitors.
- Concentrate on an unserved, poorly served, or emerging market segment that represents growth and, in turn, could help you launch into additional market segments.
- Introduce a product (or product modification) not already developed by existing competitors that can fortify your position and reinforce your concentration strategy.
- Secure your primary segment by private labeling your product concurrent with establishing your own brand. You thereby create a barrier by blocking a competitor's entry.
- Expand into additional market segments with new product offerings. Also consider modifying existing products,

providing value-added services, building-in specialized applications, or developing creative packaging.

- Recognize that every market segment you enter is actually the starting point of a new operation and a new sales cycle, which opens up a whole set of fresh possibilities.
- No campaign is complete without first determining where to concentrate your efforts. Your aim is to apply maximum effort at a decisive point. That point means positioning your resources to satisfy market demands. At the same time, you are preempting your competitor from taking similar action with any chance of success.

Finally, when developing a concentration strategy, here are strategy questions you should address:

Should you change the allocation of your resources after you have gained a favorable market position?

If you gained a dominant position, then you should move partially from the offensive to the defensive, making certain that you have an active defense against expansion-minded competitors.

You saw the effect of a somewhat lethargic response by Xerox's management when Japanese copier companies first showed interest in the North American market and then moved energetically to concentrate in the small business segment as its initial point of entry.

Consequently, how you deploy your resources and, in particular, how you shape your marketing mix should change with the situation. That also means adding as much flexibility to your organization as feasible, which includes holding reserves. You thereby ready yourself to respond rapidly to counter competitors' moves.

Also, one of the essential activities related to properly allocating resources is to acquire as much competitor intelligence as possible. It is from such information that you pinpoint funds for products that could successfully challenge competitors' entries. You are then able to more effectively deploy sales people, motivate middlemen, and budget promotional money.

Bottom line: As you concentrate your resources, you thereby secure an advantage of forcing a competitor to spread his efforts and weaken his overall market position.

How will your personnel react under diverse market conditions and during actual competitive confrontations?

The straightforward answer is that only the skilled will survive. The actions of personnel under a variety of circumstances should continuously remain top of mind and your primary concern.

Therefore, as indicated earlier the quality of your individuals is far superior to quantity. Consequently, don't sacrifice quality. If you do, there is failure – unless the competition is far inferior to yours.

While no situation offers certain results, it is clear that those with the skills and high-level training can turn shortcomings to an advantage. Conversely, those who lack skills are in jeopardy. The ultimate responsibility for the condition of your personnel remains with you. And it deserves your highest priority. It is an essential factor in leadership and managerial capability.

Are you prepared for changes in your personnel's behavior if the competitive situation shifts from success to failure?

Determine from past performance how your personnel behaved before, during, and after a tough market encounter. For instance, were there signs of order or disorder if business plans started to crumble? Specifically, was there a point at which personnel were ready to retreat?

Was there an instance where managers were able to resume control? Also, how were managers perceived by those they supervised?

Find out if communication channels were intact and did they lead to understanding or confusion. Find out what were the unspoken or disguised messages that generated encouragement or discouragement, elation, or fear.

What can be said about all these points with reference to the competitor?

Since the best long-term strategy cannot produce good results if short-term tactics are at fault, how do you assess your overall performance compared with that of your competitor?

Look at how your people performed under a variety of market scenarios. Also determine how they reacted to being managed.

All too often, it is not the underlings that are at fault. Rather, managers must take full blame in such areas as: incompetent leadership, poor or non-existent market and competitive intelligence, inadequate or unclear communications, ignorance of fundamental strategy rules, and an inability to motivate employees to implement plans with speed and enthusiasm.

SCREENING A MARKET SEGMENT

There is a reliable and systematic procedure to help in selecting segments. It consists of formal models that use a variety of criteria to rate the attractiveness of market segments. They can be used by all size firms to make investment decisions on a market-by-market or product-by-product basis.

Whereas various screening grids exist to determine the viability of the market segment, one of the long-lasting and popular ones is the **General Electric Business Screen**. It consists of a comprehensive, multifactor analysis that provides graphic display of where a business unit, product line, or market segment fits competitively in relation to a variety of criteria.

The GE Business Screen provides immeasurable help in systematically selecting a market segment, analyzing the competitive situation, and developing marketing strategies.

> ***Key point:***
>
> Screening tools can add greater precision to your decisions – and assist you in allocating resources to market segments and products for the greatest return.

The key points in using the GE Business Screen include:

1. *Industry attractiveness*, which is shown on the vertical axis of the grid in Figure 7.1. It is based on rating such factors as market size, market growth, pricing, market diversity, competitive structure, industry profitability, technical role, social issues, environment, legal, and human factors.
   Each factor is then given a weight of high, medium, or low in overall attractiveness to classify an industry, market segment, or product.
2. *Business strength* is shown on the horizontal axis. A weighted rating is made for such factors as growth, relative market share, position, margins, technology position, strengths/weaknesses, image, pollution, people, competitiveness, product quality, knowledge of customer and market, sales effectiveness, and geography.
   The results would show your ability to compete and, in turn, provide insight into developing favorable strategies in relation to competitors. In both categories, you can customize the rating factors to suit your business and industry.
3. Three-color sectors divide the grid into green, yellow, and red:

The *green sector* has three cells at the upper left and indicates those markets that are favorable in industry attractiveness and business strength. These markets have a "green light" to move in aggressively.

The *yellow sector* includes the diagonal cells stretching from the lower left to upper right. This sector indicates a medium level in overall attractiveness and indicates a level of caution.

The *red sector* covers the three cells in the lower right. This sector indicates those markets that are low in overall attractiveness and signals a stop in activity, unless there are long-term strategic reasons to remain; or there is a need to provide a defense to your main business.

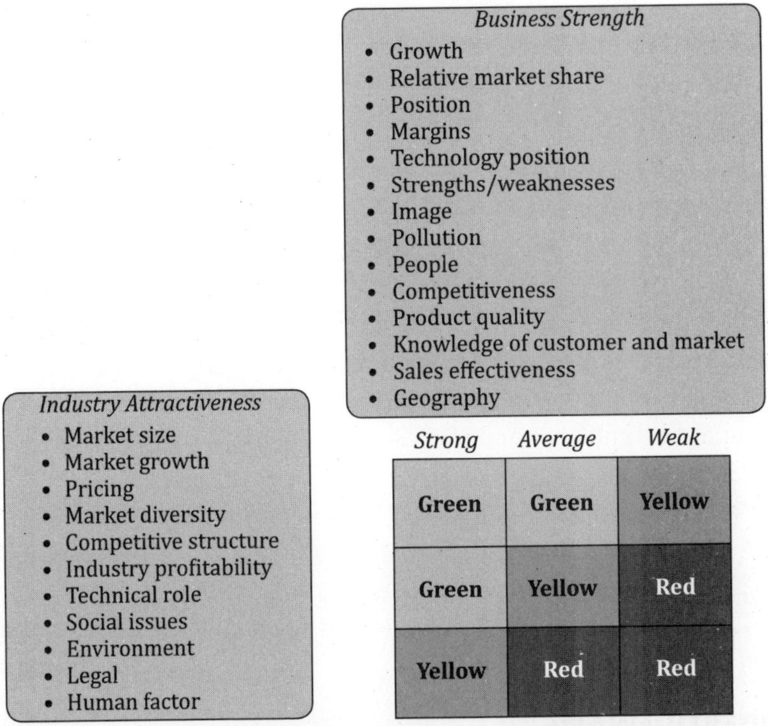

Figure 7.1. General Electric Business Screen

There is one final approach to segmentation management, which is an extension of the screening process. The approach calls for conducting a comprehensive strength/weakness analysis.

You can use the 100-question checklist that follows as is, or modify the questions to suit your industry and business. It is the definitive technique as you make the hard decisions to pursue, retain, or defend a market.

STRENGTH/WEAKNESS ANALYSIS

The checklist serves as a finite check of your business in two ways:

1. You analyze those key factors – market, customers, competitors – that affect your ability to carry out your business plans.

2. You assess your company's internal competencies to determine what strategies can be used to take advantage of opportunities.

For best results, form a team to provide objective answers to the questions. If you can't answer all the questions, then move on. You will still gain valuable insights about strengths and weaknesses, which will reveal actions you need to take.

Also, the work will seem easier if you and members of your group can keep in mind that the purpose of this time-consuming task is to develop growth opportunities that will ultimately impact positively on individuals and the company – particularly in tough competitive and economic times.

> ***Key point:***
>
> The purpose of a strength/weakness analysis is to develop competitive strategies and thereby create competitive advantage.

QUESTIONNAIRE

Part I: Reviewing Your Firm's Market Environment

Consumers

1. Who are your ultimate buyers?
2. Who or what influences them in their buying decisions?
3. What are your consumers' demographic and psychographic profiles?
4. When, where, and how do they shop for and consume your product?
5. What need(s) does your product satisfy?
6. How well does it satisfy?
7. How can you best segment your target market?
8. How do prospective buyers perceive your product?
9. What are the economic conditions of your target market?
10. Are your consumers' attitudes, values, or buying habits changing?

Customers

11. Who are your intermediate customers, if any, e.g., wholesalers and/or retailers?
12. Who or what influences them in their decision to carry your product?
13. Where are your customers located?
14. What competitive products do they carry?
15. What is their size, and what percentage of your total revenue does each customer represent?
16. How well do they serve you along the supply chain?
17. How well do you serve their needs?
18. How much support do they give your product?
19. What made you select them and they select you?
20. How can you motivate them to work harder for you?
21. Do you need them?
22. Do they need you?
23. Do you use multiple channels of distribution?
24. Would you be better off setting up your own distribution system?
25. Should you go direct?

Competitors

26. Who are your competitors?
27. Where are they located?
28. How big are they overall and, specifically, in your product area and market segment?
29. What is their product mix?
30. Is their participation in this field growing or declining? What are their primary strengths and weaknesses?
31. Which competitors may be leaving the field?
32. What new domestic competitors may be on the horizon?
33. What new off-shore competitors may be on the horizon?
34. Which competitive strategies and tactics appear particularly successful or unsuccessful?
35. What new directions is the competition pursuing?

Other Relevant Factors

36. What are the legal constraints affecting your business plans?
37. To what extent does government regulation restrict your flexibility in making market-related decisions?
38. What requirements do you have to meet?
39. What political or legal developments are looming that will improve or worsen your situation?
40. What threats or opportunities does technological progress hold in store for you?
41. How well do you keep up with technology?
42. What broad cultural shifts are occurring that may affect your business?
43. What consequences will demographic and geographic shifts have for your business?
44. Are any changes in resource availability foreseeable?
45. How do you propose to cope with environmental constraints and the "green" movement?

Part II: Reviewing Management Procedures and Policies

Analysis

46. What type of a research function do you have to monitor the market and competition? Is it adequate? How can it be improved?
47. Do you conduct regular and systematic market analysis?
48. Do you subscribe to any regular market data service?
49. Do you test and retest carefully before you introduce a new product?
50. Are all your major marketing decisions based on solidly researched facts?

Planning

51. How carefully do you examine and how aggressively do you cope with problems, difficulties, challenges, and threats to your business?

52. How do you identify and capitalize on opportunities in your marketplace?
53. What approaches are used to determine major gaps in needs?
54. Do you develop clearly stated and prioritized short-term and long-term objectives?
55. What are your planning objectives?
56. Are your objectives achievable and measurable?
57. Do you have a formalized annual business planning procedure?
58. Do you manage by objectives?
59. What is your core strategy for achieving your objectives?
60. Are you employing a push (through intermediaries) or pull (through consumers) as a strategy?
61. To what extent are you considering diversification or joint ventures?
62. How effectively are you segmenting your target market?
63. Are you allocating sufficient or excessive resources to accomplish your objectives?
64. Are your resources optimally allocated to the major elements of your marketing mix (product, price, promotion, distribution?)
65. How well do you tie in your marketing plan with the other functional plans of your organization?

Implementation and Control

66. Is your business plan truly followed or just filed away?
67. Do you continuously monitor your environment to determine the adequacy of your plan?
68. Do you use controls and checkpoints to monitor your objectives?
69. Do you compare planned to actual figures periodically and take appropriate measures if they differ significantly?
70. Do you systematically study the contribution and effectiveness of various activities, e.g., marketing and technology?

Organization

71. Does your firm involve a senior-level person to participate in planning and overseeing the implementation of the business plan?
72. How capable and motivated are your personnel?
73. Is there a need for more training, incentives, supervision, or evaluation?
74. Is your company properly organized to best serve the needs of different marketing activities, product development, target markets, and sales territories?
75. Does your entire organization embrace and practice relationship marketing with a total customer-driven orientation?

Part III: Reviewing Strategy

Product Policy

76. What is the makeup of your product mix and how well are its components selling?
77. Does it have optimal breadth and depth?
78. Should any of your products be phased out?
79. Do you carefully evaluate any negative ripple effects on the remaining product mix before you make a decision to phase-out a product?
80. Have you considered modification, repositioning, and/or extension of sagging products?
81. What additions, if any, should be made to your product mix?
82. Which products are you best equipped to make yourselves and which items should you buy and resell under your own company or brand name?
83. Do you routinely check product safety and product liability?
84. Do you have a formalized and tested product recall procedure?
85. Is any recall imminent?

Pricing

86. To what degree are your prices based on cost, demand, and/or competitive considerations?
87. How would your customers react to higher or lower prices?
88. Do you use temporary price promotions and, if so, how effective are they?
89. Do you suggest resale prices?
90. How do your wholesale or retail margins and discounts compare with those of the competition and your industry?

Promotion

91. Do you state your advertising objectives clearly?
92. How do you determine an advertising budget: a) based on last year's spending, b) a percentage of sales, or c) the preferred approach of determining what funds are needed to achieve the objective?
93. Are your advertising copy themes effective?
94. Is your media mix optimal and have you assessed the potential of the Internet with all its expanding social networking possibilities?
95. Do you make aggressive use of sales promotion techniques?

Personal Selling and Distribution

96. Is your sales force (if any) at the right strength to accomplish your marketing objectives and to what extent will the Internet affect your sales force?
97. Is it optimally organized according to geographic, market, or product criteria?
98. Is it adequately trained and motivated, and characterized by high morale, ability, and effectiveness?
99. Have you optimized your distribution setup, or are there opportunities for further streamlining?
100. Is your customer service meeting the needs of your customers?

SUMMARY OF KEY POINTS

- Search for opportunities in unserved, poorly served, or emerging market segments. When identified, selectively penetrate and expand the most promising niches by improving products and services, stretching product lines, and positioning your product to the needs of customers and against competitors.
- Identify ways to create new opportunities in segments by participating in promising new technologies and innovations. Along with others in your group, try to pioneer something new or unique. Explore joint venture and various forms of alliances where you do not have resources to access new technologies.
- Monitor changing behavioral patterns and preferences. For instance, practice segmenting a market according to evolving purchasing patterns, such as through the Internet. Also, identify clusters of customers who might buy or utilize different services for different reasons.
- Learn how your competitors segment their markets; what products and services they offer; what strategies they pursue; and how they promote, distribute, and price.

The following chapter takes you through the planning process. Here is where all the guidelines, techniques, and methods from the previous chapters converge into a strategic business plan that leads you forward into opportunities and growth.

8

Create an Effective Business Plan

The Strategic Business Plan (SBP) is the "housing" for all your objectives, market intelligence, and ultimately the business-building strategies that will set your plan in motion.

With the forms and guidelines that follow, you can develop your personalized plan while retaining the planning structure of a proven format. Meaning: You have the flexibility to customize the forms by inserting the specific terminology, vocabulary, and unique issues related to your company and industry.

Also, you can make the SBP a permanent part of your management operating system by scanning this entire planning format into your computer. Doing so permits you to add special forms required by your organization or insert many of the commercially available spreadsheet programs, as well as the growing number of Customer Relationship Management (CRM) programs.

As you develop your SBP, keep in mind the rules of competitive strategy presented in this Website. Use them as a continuing guide. They will help you strengthen the plan and ultimately increase the likelihood for creating new opportunities.

One special planning tip: If you lack specific information to answer a question, either skip the question or use your best intuitive response. In no case give up; keep the process going by moving on to the next item.

OVERVIEW OF THE STRATEGIC BUSINESS PLAN: STRATEGIC SECTION

You can obtain optimum results for your SBP by following the process diagrammed in Figure 8.1. As you examine the flowchart, notice that the top row of boxes represents the strategic portion of the plan and covers a three to five year timeframe.

The second row of boxes displays the tactical one-year plan. It is the merging of the strategic plan and tactical plan into one unified SBP that makes it a complete format and an operational management tool to energize your company's potential.

The SBP process will add an organized and disciplined approach to your thinking. Yet, in no way does it confine your thinking or creativity. Instead, the process expands your flexibility, extends your strategy vision, and elevates the innovative process. In turn, the resulting strategies provide you with a choice of revenue-building opportunities expressed through markets, products, and services.

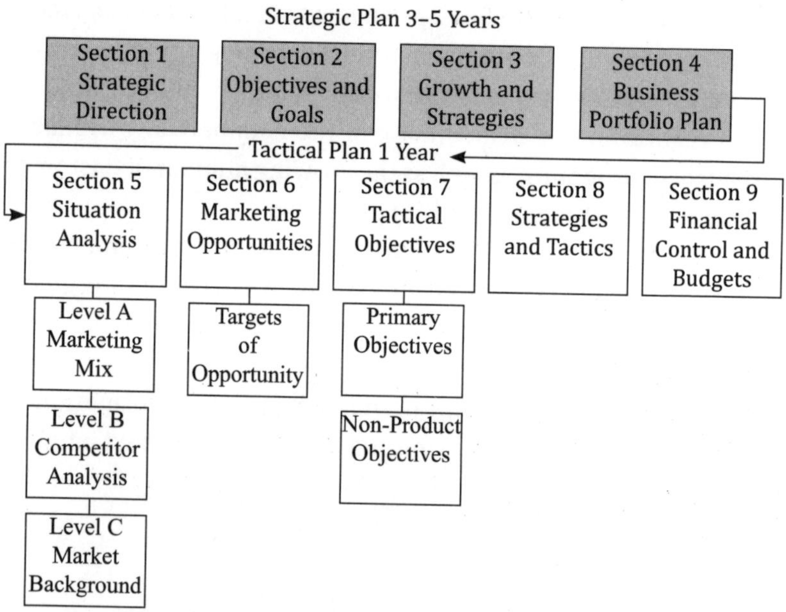

Figure 8.1. Strategic Business Plan

SECTION 1: STRATEGIC DIRECTION

The first box in Figure 8.1, Section 1, Strategic Direction, allows you to visualize the long-term direction of your company, product, or service.

Planning Guidelines

The following six questions provide an organized approach for you to develop a strategic direction. Your answers will help shape a vision of what your company, business unit, or product/service will look like over the next three to five years.

1. What are your firm's distinctive areas of expertise? This question refers to your organization's special competencies. The following list will trigger your thinking and help you develop an answer:
    - Product or service strengths based on customer satisfaction, profitability, and market share
    - Your relationships within the supply chain/or with end-use customers
    - Existing production capabilities
    - Technology advantages
    - Size of your sales force
    - Financial strength
    - R&D and other product development initiatives
    - Amount of customer or technical services provided
    - Unique skills of personnel
    - A corporate culture favorable to supporting the SBP

Fill in:

____

____

____

2. What business should your firm be in over the next 3 to 5 years? In what ways do you see it being different from what your company or business unit looks like today?

____

____

____

3. What new segments or categories of customers will you serve?

____

____

____

4. What additional functions, products, or services will you likely offer customers as you see the market evolve?

____

____

____

5. What new technologies will you require to satisfy future customer and market needs?

____

____

____

6. What changes will likely take place in any of the following areas that will impact your company: evolving markets, consumer behavior and buying patterns, availability of resources, domestic and off-shore competition, the Internet, environmental (green) issues, trade practices, and the economy? Add any other changes

unique to your company or industry that will likely affect your business.

Now compress your answers to the above six questions into one statement that would represent a realistic Strategic Direction for your company, business unit, or product.

As you develop your Strategic Direction, recognize that your corporate culture is the operating system and nerve center of your organization. Therefore, make certain that your company's culture can support your vision.

The following statement is an actual example of a well-written Strategic Direction with an expansive vision for growth in a changing marketplace:

"Our strategic direction is to meet the needs of consumers and healthcare providers for drug-delivery devices by offering a full line of hypodermic products and product systems. Our leadership position will be maintained through internal research and development, licensing of technology, and/or acquisitions to provide alternative administration and monitoring systems."

The company's previous statement indicated a narrower and highly restrictive vision, which left it vulnerable to low-cost producers and with little room for opportunistic thinking and growth:

"Our position is to be a leader in the manufacture of hypodermic needles."

SECTION 2: OBJECTIVES AND GOALS

Planning Guidelines

State your objectives and goals both quantitatively and nonquantitatively (the second box in the top row of Figure 8.1).

Your primary guideline: Still using a timeframe of 3 to 5 years, look again at your Strategic Direction, and then develop objectives that will have a wide-ranging impact on the growth of your business.

Quantitative Objectives

Indicate major performance expectations such as: sales growth, market share, return on investment, profit, and any other quantitative objectives required by your company.

With this longer timeframe, your objectives are generally broad and relate to the total business or to a few major market segments. (In the tactical section these objectives will be more specific for each product and market.)

____

____

____

Nonquantitative Objectives

Think of these objectives as a means to build-on to your organization's existing strengths or core competencies - or to eliminate any internal weaknesses.

Above all, keep your objectives specific, actionable, realistic, and focused on developing opportunities and achieving a sustainable competitive advantage.

Use the following examples to trigger objectives for your business:

- Improve supply-chain relationships and/or enhance the product's position on the supply chain
- Integrate the Internet and social networks into marketing plans
- Expand secondary distribution, e.g., find innovative approaches to reach customers beyond your primary methods
- Build specialty products to penetrate markets for greater market share or to discourage competitor's entry
- Establish or improve competitive intelligence procedures
- Focus training actions on improving skills, discipline, attitudes, and performance of employees
- Launch new products and reposition old ones
- Upgrade customer relationships
- Expand technical services
- Improve marketing mix (product, price, promotion, and distribution) management

____

____

____

____

SECTION 3: GROWTH STRATEGIES

Planning Guidelines

This section outlines the process you use to accomplish your objectives and goals. Think of strategies as actions to achieve your longer-term objectives; tactics as actions to achieve shorter-term objectives.

Since this timeframe covers 3 to 5 years, strategies are indicated here. The one-year portion, illustrated later in the plan, identifies tactics.

In practice, where you have developed broad-based, long-term objectives you should list multiple strategies for achieving each objective. In instances where you find it difficult to apply specific strategies, it is appropriate to use general strategy statements.

Suggestion: How you write your strategies can vary according to your individual or team's style. For example, you can restate each objective from Section 2, followed by a listing of corresponding strategies.

Still another option is to write a general strategy statement followed by a detailed listing of specific objectives and corresponding strategies.

The key point: Each objective (what you want to accomplish) must be followed by one or more strategies (actions to reach your objective.)

As an additional guideline, your thinking about strategies should take into account actions related to many of the following categories:

- Markets in different stages of the life cycle – introduction, growth, maturity, or decline
- Brand development and product positioning
- Product quality and value-added options
- Market share expansion
- Supply chain options
- Product, price, promotion mix, including the Internet
- Financing and asset allocations
- Specific marketing, technology, and manufacturing strengths to be exploited
- Employee training and development
- Corporate culture, people management, and internal operating systems

SECTION 4: BUSINESS PORTFOLIO PLAN

Planning Guidelines

The business portfolio includes listings of existing products and markets, as well as new products and markets. Following a logical progression, it is based on the strategic direction, objectives and goals, and growth strategies outlined in the previous sections.

In particular, your portfolio should mirror your strategic direction. That is, the broader the scope of your strategic direction, the more expansive the range of products and markets in the portfolio.

Conversely, the narrower the dimension of your strategic direction, the more limited the content of products and markets.

Use the following format and guidelines to develop your own business portfolio:

Existing Products/Existing Markets (Market Penetration)

List those existing products you currently offer to existing customers or market segments. In an appendix of the SBP, you can document in numerical or graphic form sales, profits, market share data, and other pertinent facts related to growth potential or competitive issues.

From such information you can determine if your level of penetration is adequate and if possibilities exist for further growth.

New Products/Existing Markets (Product Development)

In this section extend your thinking and list potential new products/services you can offer to existing markets. Again, recall the guideline that the broader the dimension of your Strategic Direction the broader the possibilities for the content of your portfolio. Also, continue thinking in a timeframe of 3 to 5 years.

___

___

___

Existing Products/New Markets (Market Development)

Now list your existing products into new markets. Explore possibilities for market development by identifying emerging, neglected, or poorly served segments in which existing products can be utilized.

___

___

___

New Product/New Markets (Diversification)

This portion of the business portfolio is somewhat visionary, since it involves developing new products for new and yet-untapped markets. Consider new technologies, global markets, the green trend, and potential alliances.

Once again, interpret your Strategic Direction in its broadest context. Do not seek diversification for its own sake. Rather, the whole purpose of the exercise is for you to develop an organized framework for meaningful expansion.

___

___

___

After identifying any new opportunities, it may be necessary for you to revisit Section 3 (Growth Strategies) and list actions you would take to implement the opportunities.

The Business Portfolio completes the strategic portion of your SBP. Now you are ready to proceed to the one-year tactical plan.

THE STRATEGIC BUSINESS PLAN TACTICAL SECTION

Overview

The tactical plan, the second row of boxes in Figure 8.1, designated as Sections 5 through 9, is not a stand-alone plan. It is an integral part of the total SBP.

Where commonalties exist among similar products and markets, one tactical plan can work as long as you make the appropriate changes in such areas as the sales force and the communications mix. Where you face substantial differences in the character of your products and markets, then develop separate tactical plans.

Suggestion: Avoid the temptation to develop your plan by jumping into the middle of the SBP and beginning the planning process with the one-year tactical plan. There are no suitable short cuts. Reason: Input to the tactical plan flows from two directions:

(1) From the strategic portion of the SBP (top row); and

(2) from the situation analysis (second row), which progresses to opportunities, annual objectives, tactics, and budgets.

Also, the thought process that went into the strategic portion of the plan should now flow down to feed the shorter-term, action-oriented tactical plan.

SECTION 5: SITUATION ANALYSIS

The following 3-part situation analysis details the past and current situations of your business:

Level A: Marketing Mix (product, price, distribution, and promotion)
Level B: Competitor Analysis
Level C: Market Background

The purpose of the Situation Analysis is to define your business in a factual and objective manner. Compile historical data for a period of at least 3 years. Doing so provides an excellent perspective about where your company has been, where it is now, and where you want it to go as defined in your Strategic Direction (Section 1.)

Level A: Marketing Mix – Product

Planning Guidelines

- Objectively describe the performance of your product or service by: sales history, profitability, share of market, and any other required metrics. Where appropriate, chart sales history with spreadsheets, graphics, or your company's forms.

____

____

____

- Explain the product's current position as it relates to market penetration, reputation, and competitiveness. Also, indicate where the product is in its life cycle, e.g., introduction, growth, maturity, or decline.

____

____

____

- Identify future trends as they relate to such areas as the environment, industry, customers, and competitive factors that may affect future prospects.

____

____

____

- Indicate the intended purpose of your product in terms of its applications or uniqueness.

____

____

____

- Describe features and benefits of your product as related to quality, performance, reliability, safety, convenience, and other factors important to customers.

____

____

____

- List other pertinent product information such as expected product improvements and additional product characteristics (size, model, price, packaging); recent features that enhance the product's position; trends in features, benefits, technological changes; and changes that would add superior value to the product and provide a competitive advantage.

____

____

____

Level A: Marketing Mix – Pricing

History of Pricing

Examine the history of pricing strategies for each market segment and describe its impact on the product's market position.

Future Pricing Trends

Indicate pricing trends as they pertain to new product features, expected market changes, trade and consumer reactions, and competitive responses to your pricing strategies.

Level A: Marketing Mix – Distribution

Current Channels

Describe the make-up of your supply chain. Identify the functions performed at each stage within the network (distributor, dealer, direct, e-commerce.) Indicate levels of performance, expressed in sales volume, profitability, and percentage of business increases.

Where appropriate, also analyze your physical distribution system, such as warehouse locations, inventory systems, or just-in-time delivery procedures.

Effectiveness of Coverage

Characterize the effectiveness of coverage by the programs and services provided for each channel.

Comment on effectiveness of the supply chain. Specify the key activities performed at each point and indicate any areas that require corrective action. Also comment on the impact of future trends in supply chain management, including e-commerce.

___

___

___

Future Trends

Indicate future trends in supply chain management and how they would affect various links in the chain. Also, describe trends in e-commerce and any new methods of physical distribution.

___

___

___

Level A: Marketing Mix – Advertising, Sales Promotion, Internet, Publicity, Sales

Planning Guidelines

Evaluate your efforts directed at each market segment or distribution channel based on the following: expenditures, creative strategy, social media, types of promotion, Internet, and other forms of communications unique to your industry.

___

___

___

Sales Force Functions

List functions performed by your company's (or distributor's) sales force. Indicate their effect on various market segments. If applicable, comment on such approaches as a "push" strategy (through distributors) or a "pull" strategy (through end-users.)

Key Accounts

List key accounts and their levels of performance. Comment on their contributions to long-term growth, sales, and profits. Add any comments related to providing special sales activities to retain them.

Strategies

Identify your company's past and current communications strategies by product and market segment and describe trends in these areas.

Other Support Strategies

Identify other support programs (publicity, educational, professional, trade shows, webinars, literature, films/videos, social networks) that you have used and evaluate their effectiveness.

Competitive Trends

Identify and evaluate competitive trends in the same categories as above. Look at off-shore as well as domestic competitors.

____

____

____

Planning Guidelines

Level B: Competitor Analysis

Make your competitive analysis as comprehensive as possible. The more competitive intelligence you gather, the more strategy options you have open to you.

Market Share

List all your competitors in descending-size order along with their sales and market shares, if applicable. Include your company's ranking within the listing. Show at least three competitors, more if the information is meaningful.

(If unable to provide useable information for this portion, you should give high priority to developing a competitor intelligence effort.)

____

____

____

Competitors' Strengths and Weaknesses

Identify each competitor's strengths and weaknesses related to such factors as product development, distribution, pricing, promotion, management leadership, caliber of employees, and financial condition.

Also indicate any significant trends that would signal unsettling market situations, such as aggressive moves by a competitor to grow market share or use excessive discounting to maintain its market position.

___

___

___

Product Competitiveness

Identify competitive pricing strategies, including discount practices, if any. Identify those competitors firmly entrenched in low-price segments of the market, those at the high end of the market, or competitors that are low-cost producers.

___

___

___

Product Features and Benefits

Compare the specific features and benefits of your product against those of competitive products. In particular, focus on product quality, design factors, and performance. Evaluate price/value relationships for each, discuss customer preferences, and identify unique product innovations.

___

___

___

Advertising Effectiveness

Identify competitive spending levels and their effectiveness, as measured by awareness levels, competitive copy claims, and reach/frequency levels (if available.)

Such measurements are often conducted by advertising agencies, marketing research firms, or some publications. If you cannot use these sources, rely on informal observation and whatever measurements you can obtain.

____

____

____

Effectiveness of the Supply Chain

Compare competitive distribution strengths and weaknesses. Address differences in market penetration, market coverage, delivery time, and physical movement of the product by regions or territories.

____

____

____

Packaging

Compare packaging based on performance, innovation, and customer preference. Also review size, shape, function, convenience of handling, ease of storage, and shipping.

____

____

____

Trade/Consumer Attitudes

Review both trade and consumer attitudes toward product quality, warranties, customer/technical service, company image, and company performance.

____

____

____

Competitive Share of Market Trends

Specify trends in market share by individual products, as well as by market segments. Further, identify where each competitor is making a major commitment and where it may be relinquishing control by product and segment.

Sales Force Effectiveness and Market Coverage

Compare effectiveness by sales, service, frequency of contact, and problem-solving capabilities by competitor and by market segment against your own performance. Also, look at all sales force performance within the supply chain.

Planning Guidelines

Level C: Market Background

This last part of the situation analysis focuses on the demographic and behavioral factors of your market. Here is where you determine market size and customer preferences – both business-to-business and business-to-consumer.

If you give careful attention to compiling accurate information, you can provide useful input to the following parts of the SBP: Section 6, Marketing Opportunities; Section 7, Tactical Objectives; and Section 8, Strategies and Tactics.

This information also highlights any gaps in knowledge about markets and customers, which helps you determine what additional market intelligence is needed to make more effective decisions.

Fill-in the following categories as part of the market background:

Customer Profile

Describe existing and potential customers that you or your distributors serve. Profile them by type of products used, level of service required, price sensitivity, and promotional support.

Also look at customer purchases by frequency, volume, and seasonality of purchase. Additional information might include issues related to maintaining customer inventory levels, just-in-time delivery, retail-stocking policies, and volume discounts. Also consider e-commerce and any resulting impact on buying behavior.

___

___

___

Geographic Aspects of Products Used

Define customer purchases by region and any territory limitations you encounter.

___

___

___

Market Characteristics

Also assess the demographic, psychographic (lifestyle), and other relevant characteristics of your customers. Look at purchase patterns and any distinctive behavioral styles, as well as attitudes toward your company's products, services, quality, and image.

___

___

___

Decision Maker

Define who makes the buying decisions and when and where they are made. Identify the various individuals or departments that may influence the decision.

____

____

____

Customer Motivations

Identify the key motivations that drive your customers to buy your product. Why do they select you over a competitor?

Customers may buy your product because of quality, performance, price, company image, technical/customer service, convenience, location, delivery, access to upper-level management, friendship, or peer pressure.

____

____

____

Customer Awareness

Define the level of consumer awareness of your products. To what extent do they:

- Recognize a need for your product?
- Identify your product, brand, or company as a possible supplier?
- Associate your product, brand, or company with desirable features?

____

____

____

Segment Trends

Define trends in the size and character of the various segments or niches you serve. A segment should be considered if it is accessible, measurable, potentially profitable, and has long-term growth potential.

Segmenting a market also serves as an offensive strategy to identify emerging, neglected, or poorly served markets that can catapult you to further sales growth.

You can also consider segments as a defensive strategy to prevent inroads of a potential competitor through an unattended market segment.

____

____

____

Other Comments or Critical Issues

Add general comments or references that would contribute to your knowledge of the market and customer base. Also list any critical issues that have surfaced as a result of conducting the situation analysis – ones that should be singled out for special attention.

____

____

____

SECTION 6: MARKET OPPORTUNITIES

Planning Guidelines

In this section, you examine strengths, weaknesses, and options. Opportunities will begin to emerge as you consider a variety of alternatives.

Try to avoid restricted thinking. Take your time and brainstorm. Dig for opportunities with other members of your planning team. If one doesn't exist, then put together a team representing different functional areas of the business.

Consider all possibilities for expanding existing market coverage and laying the groundwork for entering new markets. Also consider opportunities related to your competition. For instance, offensively, which competitors can you displace from which market segments? Defensively, which competitors can you deny entry into your market?

As you go through this section, revisit your strategic portion of the SBP (top row of boxes in Figure 8.1.) Also refer to the situation analysis in the last section, specifically the competitive analysis, which would reveal voids or weaknesses that could turn into opportunities.

Use the following screening process to identify your major opportunities and challenges. Once you identify and prioritize the opportunities, convert them into objectives and tactics, which are the action topics of the next two sections of the SBP.

Present Markets

Identify the best opportunities for expanding present markets by:

- Cultivating an additional revenue stream through new users
- Displacing competition
- Increasing product usage or services by present customers

- Redefining market segments
- Reformulating or repackaging the product
- Identifying new applications for the product
- Repositioning the product to create a more favorable perception by consumers, and by developing a competitive advantage over rival products
- Expanding into emerging, neglected, or poorly served market niches

Targets of Opportunity

List any areas outside your current market segment or product line not included in the above categories that you would like to explore. Be innovative and entrepreneurial in your thinking.

These areas are opportunistic. Therefore, due to their innovative and risky characteristics, they are isolated from the other opportunities. Those you select for special attention are placed in a separate part of the objectives section of the SBP.

SECTION 7: TACTICAL OBJECTIVES

Now set the objectives you want to achieve during the current planning cycle – generally defined as a 12-month period to correspond with annual budgeting procedures.

Once again, you will find it useful to review Sections 5 and 6. Also, it will be helpful to review the strategic portion of the plan. You want to be certain that selective actions related to your long-range strategic direction, objectives, strategies, and the business portfolio are incorporated into your tactical one-year objectives.

This section consists of three parts:

- Assumptions: projections about future conditions and trends
- Primary objectives: metrics related to what you want to accomplish, including targets of opportunity
- Functional objectives: operational goals representing various parts of the business

Planning Guidelines

Assumptions

For objectives to be realistic and achievable, you must first generate assumptions and projections about future conditions and trends. List only those major assumptions that will affect your business for the planning period.

- Economic assumptions:

Comment on the overall economy, local market economies, consumer expenditures, and changes in customer buying patterns. Also document any impact on market size, growth rate, costs, and trends in your market segments.

____

____

____

- Technological assumptions:

Include likelihood of technological breakthroughs and applications of new technology to your business.

___

___

___

- Sociopolitical assumptions:

Indicate any positive and restrictive legislation, political tensions, tax outlook, population patterns, educational factors, and changes in customer habits linked to social media and e-commerce.

___

___

___

- Competitive assumptions:

Identify activities of existing competitors, inroads of new competitors, with particular attention to surging global competitors, and subsequent changes in trade practices.

___

___

___

Planning Guidelines

Primary Objectives

Focus on the primary financial objectives that your organization requires. Also include targets of opportunity that you initially identified as innovative and entrepreneurial in Section 6.

Where there are multiple objectives you may find it helpful to rank them in priority order. Be sure to use metrics to quantify expected results where possible. You can separate your objectives into the following categories:

- Primary objectives

Current and projected sales, profits, market share, return on investment, and other quantitative measures. (Use either Table 8.1, forms provided by your organization, or any commercial spreadsheet software.)

Table 8.1. Primary Objectives

	Current				Projected			
Product Group Breakdown	Sales ($)	Units	Margins	Share of Market	Sales ($)	Units	Margins	Share of Market
Product A								
Product B								
Product C								
Product D								

- Targets of opportunity objectives

Planning Guidelines

Functional Objectives

State the functional objectives relating to both product and nonproduct issues in each of the following categories. Should any of the categories not apply to your business, simply consider any possible application for the future, and then move on.

Product Objectives

- Quality

List quality objectives that would achieve a competitive advantage.

- Development

Indicate possibilities to acquire new technology through internal R&D, licensing, or joint ventures.

- Modification

Describe major or minor product changes through reformulation, redesign, or reengineering.

- Differentiation

Diversify into new geographic areas, such as developing markets, by altering the product and delivering new applications.

- Diversification

Transfer technology or use the actual product in new applications, or diversify into new geographic areas, such as developing markets.

- Deletion

Remove a product from the line due to unsatisfactory performance, or keep it in the line if the product serves some strategic purpose, such as presenting your company to the market as a full-line supplier.

- Segmentation

Create line extensions (adding product varieties) to reach new market niches or defend against an incoming competitor in an existing market segment.

Pricing Objectives

- Include list prices, volume discounts, and promotional rebates.

Promotion Objectives

- Develop sales force support, sales promotion, advertising, Internet, social networks, and publicity to the trade and consumers.

Supply Chain Objectives

- Add new distributors to increase geographic coverage, develop programs or services to solidify relationships with the trade, remove distributors or dealers from the chain, or maintain direct contact with the end user.

Physical Distribution Objectives

- Identify logistical factors from order entry to the physical movement of a product through the supply chain, and eventual delivery to the end user.

Packaging Objectives

- Use functional design and/or decorative considerations for brand identification.

Service Objectives

- Broaden the range of services, from providing customers access to key personnel in your firm, to providing on-site technical assistance.

Other Objectives

- Indicate other objectives as suggested in Targets of Opportunities.

Planning Guidelines

Nonproduct Objectives

Although most activities eventually relate to the product or service, some are support functions that you should consider. (Obtain input from personnel in other functions, as needed.)

- Key Accounts

Indicate those customers with whom you can develop special relationships through customized products, distribution, value-added services, or participation in quality improvement programs.

- Manufacturing

Identify special activities that would provide a competitive advantage, such as offering small production runs to accommodate the changing needs of customers and reduce inventory levels.

- Marketing Research

Cite any customer studies or market data that reveal opportunities for new revenue streams.

- Credit

Include any programs that use credit and finance as a value-added service, such as providing financial advice or offering financial assistance to customers in specific situations.

- Technical Sales Activities

Include any support activities, such as 24/7 hotline assistance or on-site consultation to solve customers' problems.

- R&D

Indicate internal research and development projects, as well as joint ventures that would complement the Strategic Direction identified in Section 1 of the SBP.

____

____

____

- Human Resource Development and Training

Identify specialized training and development programs to upgrade the skills of those individuals who are responsible for implementing the SBP.

____

____

____

- Other

Include any activities that would contribute to your organization's uniqueness, and thereby offer a competitive advantage.

____

____

____

SECTION 8: STRATEGIES AND TACTICS

Overview

Strategy is the art of coordinating the means (money, human resources, materials) to achieve the ends (profits, customer satisfaction, growth) as defined by company policy, strategic direction, and objectives.

From another perspective: Strategies are actions to achieve long-term objectives; tactics are actions to achieve short-term objectives.

Therefore, in this section strategies and tactics are identified and put into action. Responsibilities are assigned, schedules set, budgets established, and checkpoints determined.

Make sure that individuals involved with developing and implementing the plans actively participate in this section.

Planning Guidelines

Restate the functional product and nonproduct objectives from Section 7 and link them to the strategies and tactics you will use to reach each objective.

One of the reasons for restating the objectives is to clarify the frequent misunderstanding between objectives and strategies. Objectives are what you want to accomplish; strategies are actions that specify how you intend to achieve your objectives.

Note: If you state an objective and don't have a related strategy, you may not have an objective. Instead, the statement may be an action for some other objective.

Objective 1:______________________________

Strategy/Tactic ______________________________

Objective 2:______________________________

Strategy/Tactic ______________________________

Objective 3:______________________________

Strategy/Tactic ______________________________

Planning Guidelines

Summarize Strategies

Summarize the basic strategies for achieving your primary objectives. Include alternative and contingency plans should you come up against unexpected situations that prevent you from reaching your objectives.

Note: You may choose to repeat this information as an Executive Summary in the beginning of the plan.

As you develop your final strategy statement, use the following checklist to determine its completeness. Consider the following:

- Changes to the product or package, including differentiation and value-added services.
- Strategies that create a competitive advantage, along with contingency plans to block competitors' aggressive moves.
- Changes to price, discounts, or long-term contracts that impact your market share.
- Changes to advertising strategy, such as the selection of features and benefits, or copy themes to special groups.
- Strategies to reach new, poorly served, or unserved market segments.
- Promotion strategies aimed at dealer and/or distributor, consumer, and sales force.
- Internal changes in the operating systems, as well as initiatives that would better align the corporate culture with your strategies.

____

____

____

SECTION 9: FINANCIAL CONTROLS AND BUDGETS

Planning Guidelines

Having completed the strategy phase of your SBP, you must decide how you will monitor its execution. Therefore, before implementing it, develop procedures for both control (comparing actual and planned figures) and review (deciding whether planned figures should be adjusted or other corrective measures taken.)

This final section incorporates your operating budget. If your organization has reporting procedures, you should incorporate them within this section.

Included below are examples of additional reports or data sheets for you to consider. They are designed to monitor progress at key checkpoints of the plan and to permit either major shifts in strategies or simple midcourse corrections:

- Forecast models related to the industry, environment, competition and any other areas that are applicable to your company and your plan
- Sales by channel of distribution, including:
  - Inventory or out-of-stock reports
  - Average selling price (including discounts, rebates, or allowances) along the supply chain and by customer outlet
- Profit and loss statements by product
- Direct product budgets
- R&D expenses
- Administrative budget
- Spending by quarter

As an overall guideline – regardless of the forms you use – make certain that the system serves as a reliable feedback mechanism. Your interest is in maintaining explicit and timely control so you can react swiftly to impending problems. Further, it should serve as a procedure for reviewing schedules and strategies.

The only other section in your SBP is an appendix. It should include the following items:

- Relevant industry data and market research that provide information on trends, product usage, market share, and the like.
- Data on competitors' strategies, including information on their products, pricing, promotion, distribution, market position, as well as profiles of management leadership (if available).
- Details about your new product features and benefits.

In addition, various computer databases, as well as a wide variety of customized or off-the-shelf software programs are available to assist in monitoring and strengthening your plan.

Final Guideline

After completing your plan, take a thoughtful look at its key parts. For instance, review the breadth of your strategic direction, as well as the scope of both strategies and tactics.

They may contain far-reaching and unique features to propel your company forward. Yet, be absolutely certain that in addition to the physical and financial resources to implement the Strategic Business Plan it is also aligned with the culture of your organization.

That is, can your company's history, its behavioral patterns, and leadership; the attitudes, temperaments, and skills of employees; their capacity to confront aggressive competitors; and their ability to live with risk, support the plan? Also, determine if you have sufficient resources, including financial, technology, and physical to implement the plan.

Special Feature: Strategy Diagnostic Tool

Implementing competitive strategies face numerous risks. Some come from personnel, financial, or physical obstacles that exist inside your organization and prevent you from moving forward on your plans. Others result from the numerous forces coming at you in a dynamic and overly competitive marketplace.

To increase your chances of success, the goal of the *Strategy Diagnostic Tool* is to expose those obstacles and provide corrective actions. In turn, you improve your ability to create business-building opportunities.

HOW TO USE THE STRATEGY DIAGNOSTIC TOOL

Divided into *nine strategy rules*, the diagnostic tool pinpoints the primary points within each rule so that you can reliably assess their effectiveness or ineffectiveness. Doing so, gives you a consistent gauge about the likelihood of your overall strategies succeeding.

Each strategy rule consists of three parts:

- Part 1: Lists items that explain if the particular rule is functioning *effectively* and would contribute to implementing a competitive strategy successfully.
- Part 2: Describes items that signal if the rule is functioning *ineffectively* and would be detrimental to implementing a strategy successfully.
- Part 3: Provides remedial actions based on the deficiencies you uncovered in Parts 1 and 2. Included in this Part are

Executive Comments, which are quotes from executives that tie the strategy rule to real-world problems.

Now, rate each of the items in Parts 1 and 2 as *frequently, occasionally*, or *rarely*.

STRATEGY RULE 1: SHIFT TO THE OFFENSIVE

PART 1

INDICATIONS THAT STRATEGY RULE 1 FUNCTIONS EFFECTIVELY

1. You and your staff display a proactive, shift-to-the-offensive mindset when confronted with aggressive competitors.

   Frequently ☐ occasionally ☐ rarely ☐

2. You permit risk taking among your staff, with no serious repercussions for negative results.

   Frequently ☐ occasionally ☐ rarely ☐

3. You and other managers are adept at making timely maneuvers to block rivals from taking over your market position.

   Frequently ☐ occasionally ☐ rarely ☐

4. You and other managers act with boldness, which has a positive psychological impact on employee behavior and morale.

   Frequently ☐ occasionally ☐ rarely ☐

5. Your firm is organized to permit personnel to communicate, and act rapidly, on time-sensitive market opportunities.

   Frequently ☐ occasionally ☐ rarely ☐

6. Recognizing the value of your employees' knowledge, skill, and prior experience, you actively encourage them to tap their expertise for reliable decisions.

   Frequently ☐ occasionally ☐ rarely ☐

PART 2

SYMPTOMS THAT STRATEGY RULE I IS FUNCTIONING INEFFECTIVELY

1. You are stalled by a cloud of complacency and apprehension within your group, which results in a lack of fresh ideas and initiatives for growing the business.

   Frequently ☐ occasionally ☐ rarely ☐

2. Your personnel are overly preoccupied in defending an existing market position; negligible time and effort is spent searching for new market and product opportunities.

   Frequently ☐ occasionally ☐ rarely ☐

3. Other managers and staff are caught up by fear of what competitors might do. Such negative behavior brings to a standstill any effort to mount a vigorous response strategy to counter competitors' efforts.

   Frequently ☐ occasionally ☐ rarely ☐

4. You find yourself exhibiting unwarranted caution, which permeates the group and prevents you from taking action on new market opportunities.

   Frequently ☐ occasionally ☐ rarely ☐

5. The organization tends to lose its momentum.

   Frequently ☐ occasionally ☐ rarely ☐

PART 3

REMEDIAL ACTIONS BASED ON PARTS 1 AND 2

The above ratings for Parts 1 and 2 are qualitative assessments of your ability to shift to the offensive. Based on your diagnosis, use the following remedies to apply corrective actions:

- Attack complacency: Develop ready-to-implement contingency plans that you can call up to seize market opportunities or blunt competitive threats.
- Prepare for new opportunities: Use market and competitive intelligence to support decisions and reduce the risks inherent in making bold moves.
- Instill self-confidence: Conduct specialized training related to enhancing job skills, improving discipline, as well as elevating employees' self-assurance and morale.
- Regain momentum: Employ market segmentation to understand how and where to deploy resources, thereby reducing the risks of moving into heavily-defended markets.
- Encourage an entrepreneurial mindset: Require key personnel to submit ideas that would take the company into new markets, products, and services. Use the Strategic Business Plan for this purpose.
- Support a market-driven orientation: Create cross-functional strategy teams that encourage creativity and visionary thinking.
- Prepare for unexpected events: Hold reserves.

Remedies and actions:____________________________________

____

____

Executive Comments Related to Rule 1

To illustrate the practicality of Rule 1, Shift to the Offensive, the following actual quotes come from a survey of chief executives of medium and large organizations. (Company names are withheld to maintain confidentiality. The same survey is used for Executive Comments in the rules that follow.)

"We're facing an avalanche of competition and bogged down by erratic marketing."

"My company is losing momentum and losing its way."

"Need to find the way back to the market where we got creamed."

"We need to energize the product line plagued by missed opportunities, sluggish sales, and dismal profits."

STRATEGY RULE 2: MANEUVER BY INDIRECT STRATEGY

PART I

INDICATIONS THAT STRATEGY RULE 2 FUNCTIONS EFFECTIVELY

1. You intentionally integrate *indirect strategies into your business plans, thereby increasing the success rate of your efforts.

   *An indirect strategy circumvents a competitor's strong points – usually centered on product, service, price, promotion, distribution, or people – and takes actions that attack a rival's weak areas, thereby lessening resistance and maximizing the effectiveness of available resources.

   Frequently ☐ occasionally ☐ rarely ☐

2. You understand that by acquiring the skills to implement indirect strategies, you open your mind to fresh ideas. You also reduce the risks of going after market leaders, even where limited resources are available.

   Frequently ☐ occasionally ☐ rarely ☐

3. You deliberately employ indirect approaches that produce the psychological unbalancing effect of distracting the competing manager into making false moves and costly mistakes.

   Frequently ☐ occasionally ☐ rarely ☐

4. You intentionally avoid getting entangled in direct confrontations with competitors, which would result in the unnecessary draining of resources.

   Frequently ☐ occasionally ☐ rarely ☐

PART 2

SYMPTOMS THAT STRATEGY RULE 2 IS FUNCTIONING INEFFECTIVELY

1. You are inclined not to use an indirect strategy that would deliver differentiated products that outperform those of competitors.

   Frequently ☐ occasionally ☐ rarely ☐

2. You do not probe for unserved market niches where there is minimal resistance from competitors, and where opportunities exist to establish a foothold and expand into a mainstream market.

   Frequently ☐ occasionally ☐ rarely ☐

3. Personnel do not rely on competitor intelligence to formulate an indirect strategy.

   Frequently ☐ occasionally ☐ rarely ☐

4. You do not have a benchmarking system to periodically evaluate strengths, weaknesses, or best practices, which can then be used to develop competitive strategies.

   Frequently ☐ occasionally ☐ rarely ☐

5. Personnel do not actively search for new distribution channels so that they can bypass an overcrowded supply chain.

   Frequently ☐ occasionally ☐ rarely ☐

PART 3

REMEDIAL ACTIONS BASED ON PARTS 1 AND 2

The above ratings for Parts 1 and 2 are qualitative assessments of your ability to maneuver by indirect strategy. Based on your diagnosis, use the following remedies to apply corrective actions:

- Use a SWOT (strengths, weaknesses, opportunities, threats) analysis, or comparable analytical tool, to help you determine the type of indirect strategies to employ.
- Focus on your current competitive situation and compare it to the objectives you want to achieve. Doing so allows you to gauge if your indirect strategies will produce the desired results.
- Use all available sources of intelligence to interpret your market position, which would provide additional clues to the make-up of your indirect strategies.
- Find an unattended, poorly served, or emerging market segment as a prime target to implement an indirect strategy for market expansion.
- Look to the traditional marketing 4Ps of product, price, promotion, and supply chain for ideas on how to configure a strength-against-weakness mix that cannot be easily matched by competitors.

Remedies and actions:____________________________________

____

____

Executive Comments
Related to Rule 2

"Need to outmaneuver local and regional rivals and try to muscle into new markets."

"Need to keep the company from becoming an also-ran in the industry."

"We must find a way to move closer to the end-user and develop a true competitive edge."

"We must fend-off competition not only from low-cost providers, but also from competitors with more flexible products."

STRATEGY RULE 3: ACT WITH SPEED

PART I

INDICATIONS THAT STRATEGY RULE 3 FUNCTIONS EFFECTIVELY

1. You realize that overlong, dragged-out campaigns have rarely been successful. They divert interest, depress morale, and deplete resources.

   Frequently ☐ occasionally ☐ rarely ☐

2. You recognize that speed is an essential component to secure a competitive lead, which impacts on market share, product positioning, and ultimately customer relationships.

   Frequently ☐ occasionally ☐ rarely ☐

3. Your staff understands that even minor delays can result in a loss of momentum and could signal a vigilant competitor to move in and fill the void.

   Frequently ☐ occasionally ☐ rarely ☐

4. You and your staff know that a strategy that integrates speed with technology is in an excellent position to secure a competitive lead.

   Frequently ☐ occasionally ☐ rarely ☐

5. You recognize that speed adds vitality to a company's operations and acts as a catalyst for growth.

   Frequently ☐ occasionally ☐ rarely ☐

6. You understand that acting defensively to protect a market position is but a preliminary step to moving boldly and rapidly against a competitor.

   Frequently ☐ occasionally ☐ rarely ☐

PART 2

SYMPTOMS THAT STRATEGY RULE 3 IS FUNCTIONING INEFFECTIVELY

1. You and your staff fail to acknowledge that losses in market share and competitive position often result from prolonged delays when dealing with time-sensitive market conditions.

   Frequently ☐ occasionally ☐ rarely ☐

2. A general malaise exists in the organization, which results in missed opportunities.

   Frequently ☐ occasionally ☐ rarely ☐

3. Personnel lack initiative in implementing business plans with speed.

   Frequently ☐ occasionally ☐ rarely ☐

4. You are slow in preventing a product from reaching a commodity status, which often results in price wars.

   Frequently ☐ occasionally ☐ rarely ☐

5. There is a lack of vitality due to staff inexperience and lack of training, which hinders movement.

   Frequently ☐ occasionally ☐ rarely ☐

6. You are unable to act boldly and with speed – despite suitable market conditions.

   Frequently ☐ occasionally ☐ rarely ☐

7. You are unable to secure a competitive lead due to sluggishness in integrating technology into the product and distribution mix.

   Frequently ☐ occasionally ☐ rarely ☐

8. Organizational layers prolong deliberation, foster procrastination, and delay decisions.

   Frequently ☐ occasionally ☐ rarely ☐

9. There is an overall lack of urgency in developing new products.

   Frequently ☐ occasionally ☐ rarely ☐

PART 3

REMEDIAL ACTIONS BASED ON PARTS 1 AND 2

The above ratings for Parts 1 and 2 are qualitative assessments of your ability to act with speed. Based on your diagnosis, use the following remedies to apply corrective actions:

- Reduce the organizational obstacles that prevent you and your staff from increasing the speed of internal communication, as well as acquiring information from the field.

- Require selected individuals on your staff to submit timely proposals with the prime objective of creating additional revenue streams through product innovations; new technology applications; and by identifying new, unserved, or poorly-served market segments.
- Use cross-functional strategy teams to benefit from multiple backgrounds and perspectives, as well as gain buy-in to business plans.
- Seek input from managers and field personnel in pinpointing competitors' weaknesses and areas of vulnerability.
- Conduct training to breakdown internal barriers to speed.

Remedies and actions:____________________________________

____

____

Executive Comments
Related to Rule 3

"Products are late and customers are holding off purchases of existing products, which is slowing the company's revenue growth. The delays can only help the competition."

"Delayed models damaged morale and created a dramatic loss of market share."

"We must outmaneuver local and regional rivals by bringing sophistication more rapidly to the market than they can."

STRATEGY RULE 4: GROW BY CONCENTRATION

PART I

INDICATIONS THAT STRATEGY RULE 4 FUNCTIONS EFFECTIVELY

1. You recognize that concentration is a workable strategy to challenge larger competitors on a segment-by-segment approach.

   Frequently ☐ occasionally ☐ rarely ☐

2. You and others feel competent about concentrating your resources to gain a superior position in a selected market segment.

   Frequently ☐ occasionally ☐ rarely ☐

3. You use market intelligence to pinpoint a segment for initial market entry. Then use that position to roll-out toward additional growth segments.

   Frequently ☐ occasionally ☐ rarely ☐

4. You and your staff are adept at going beyond the traditional demographic and geographic segmentation approaches by employing more finite classifications to identify new or under-served segments.

   Frequently ☐ occasionally ☐ rarely ☐

5. You and others are flexible about moving out of under-performing segments and concentrating on faster growing segments.

   Frequently ☐ occasionally ☐ rarely ☐

6. You are capable of concentrating your resources against competitors' weaknesses (the indirect approach.)

   Frequently ☐ occasionally ☐ rarely ☐

7. Marketing and sales personnel are skilled at focusing products and services to suit the specific needs of their customers.

   Frequently ☐ occasionally ☐ rarely ☐

8. You understand that every market segment presents opportunities to fill market gaps, allocate resources efficiently, and exploit a rival's limitations.

   Frequently ☐ occasionally ☐ rarely ☐

PART 2

SYMPTOMS THAT STRATEGY RULE 4 IS FUNCTIONING INEFFECTIVELY

1. You are not able to accurately select market segments that represent long-term growth.

   Frequently ☐ occasionally ☐ rarely ☐

2. You tend to dissipate resources across numerous segments.

   Frequently ☐ occasionally ☐ rarely ☐

3. Your company experiences failed product launches by not building a strategy around segment needs.

   Frequently ☐ occasionally ☐ rarely ☐

4. You have not internalized the rule that to achieve an advantageous competitive position requires a strategy of concentration, rather than to expose pockets of vulnerability and spread resources.

   Frequently ☐ occasionally ☐ rarely ☐

PART 3

REMEDIAL ACTIONS BASED ON PARTS 1 AND 2

The above ratings for Parts 1 and 2 are qualitative assessments of your ability to use a strategy of concentration. Based on your diagnosis, use the following remedies to apply corrective actions:

- Install an ongoing competitor intelligence system to identify a competitor's weaknesses.
- Concentrate on a market that is emerging, neglected, or poorly served from which to expand into additional segments.
- Secure your position with dedicated services and customized products that would create barriers to competitors' entry.
- Within market segments, tailor products and services built around product differentiation, value-added services, and business solutions that exceed those of competitors.
- Conduct strategy training sessions, especially for those individuals who resist adopting a strategy of concentration.

Remedies and actions:______________________________

____

____

Executive Comments
Related to Rule 4

"Need to develop an organization to yield a new and far more competitive company."

"We need to develop small, quasi-independent units, each of which focuses on its particular market with freedom to do what it takes to win."

"We must drive down costs, while beefing up R&D and finding new places to grow."

"We have to find ways to woo back angry retailers and build the brand image among groups that were once behind the product."

STRATEGY RULE 5: PRIORITIZE COMPETITIVE INTELLIGENCE

PART I

INDICATIONS THAT STRATEGY RULE 5
FUNCTIONS EFFECTIVELY

1. An evaluation meeting takes place after each major competitive encounter, which includes (a) comparing competitors' performance against yours, (b) assessing strategies and tactics that worked or failed, and (3) identifying the most useful type of competitor intelligence.

   Frequently ☐ occasionally ☐ rarely ☐

2. You (or the company) provide adequate funding for competitive intelligence and make it a key part of the strategy development process.

   Frequently ☐ occasionally ☐ rarely ☐

3. You and others use competitive intelligence as an evaluation tool for assessing the levels of risk associated with various strategy options.

   Frequently ☐ occasionally ☐ rarely ☐

4. You use competitive benchmarking to determine areas of vulnerability compared with those of competitors.

   Frequently ☐ occasionally ☐ rarely ☐

5. You use competitive intelligence to increase accuracy in selecting markets, locating an optimum position, and determining how to defend against a competitor's intrusion.

   Frequently ☐ occasionally ☐ rarely ☐

6. You and others recognize that competitive intelligence allows for anticipating rival's moves and giving you time to outmaneuver them, thereby making the most efficient use of resources.

   Frequently ☐ occasionally ☐ rarely ☐

PART 2

SYMPTOMS THAT STRATEGY RULE 5 IS FUNCTIONING INEFFECTIVELY

1. You frequently show surprise at competitors' actions, which hampers your ability to respond correctly and rapidly.

   Frequently ☐ occasionally ☐ rarely ☐

2. At times you tend to be indecisive due to lack of real-time information about market events, which filters down and affects the attitudes and morale of your employees.

   Frequently ☐ occasionally ☐ rarely ☐

3. Personnel are inclined to exaggerate or underestimate a competitor's situation due to unreliable or insufficient back-up intelligence.

   Frequently ☐ occasionally ☐ rarely ☐

4. There is a tendency to develop product launch plans without documenting market conditions, competitors' strengths and weaknesses, as well as buyers' specific needs.

   Frequently ☐ occasionally ☐ rarely ☐

5. No workable two-way communications channel exists from the field to the home office that red-flags opportunities or threats.

   Frequently ☐ occasionally ☐ rarely ☐

PART 3

REMEDIAL ACTIONS BASED ON PARTS 1 AND 2

The above ratings for Parts 1 and 2 are qualitative assessments of your overall ability to prioritize competitive intelligence. Based on a diagnosis of your company's situation, use the following remedies to implement corrective action:

- Make competitive intelligence an integral part of the business planning process. Use it as the centerpiece for developing offensive and defensive strategies.
- Train staff from various functions, in particular the sales force, to recognize the changing dynamics of consumer needs and competitive threats and the urgency for them to actively gather reliable intelligence.
- Use a team approach to keep track of competitors' activities, with particular attention to decoding their strategies.

- Set up a procedure for competitive benchmarking to upgrade your firm's systems and processes.
- Incorporate the use of outside sources to expand the reach of your competitive intelligence activities.

Remedies and actions____________________________________

____

____

Executive Comments
Related to Rule 5

"Sluggish markets, ferocious competition, and our management's own ineptness pummeled the organization."

"Upstart clone makers beat us with low-cost products through new channels, such as the Internet, phone, and superstores."

"We need to keep the company from becoming an also-ran in the industry. But we don't have enough quality information to guide us."

STRATEGY RULE 6: TUNE-IN TO YOUR CORPORATE CULTURE

PART I

INDICATIONS THAT STRATEGY RULE 6 FUNCTIONS EFFECTIVELY

1. You acknowledge that corporate culture is the nerve center of your organization and is at the core of what makes the organization tick. You actively tune-in to your company's traditions, values, beliefs, and history.

   Frequently ☐ occasionally ☐ rarely ☐

2. You realize that your organization's culture shapes how employees think, act, and are likely to perform in a variety of competitive encounters.

   Frequently ☐ occasionally ☐ rarely ☐

3. You recognize corporate culture as the DNA that drives all competitive strategies. It serves as one of the primary determinants in selecting strategies and tactics that will likely succeed.

   Frequently ☐ occasionally ☐ rarely ☐

4. You are aware that corporate culture influences your leadership style and consequently your ability to implement business plans.

   Frequently ☐ occasionally ☐ rarely ☐

5. You acknowledge that corporate culture is one of the prime differentiators that gives your organization a unique identity among customers and competitors.

   Frequently ☐ occasionally ☐ rarely ☐

6. You utilize corporate culture to reveal the inner workings of competitors. By that means, you can predict with some accuracy how rivals will react under a variety of market conditions.

   Frequently ☐ occasionally ☐ rarely ☐

PART 2

SYMPTOMS THAT STRATEGY RULE 6 IS FUNCTIONING INEFFECTIVELY

1. Personnel operate within a closed-in and uninspiring culture that prevents them from recognizing the hard-nosed realities of global competition.

   Frequently ☐ occasionally ☐ rarely ☐

2. The existing culture is passive so that your people fail to internalize the consequences of falling behind in new technology; similarly, they do not recognize its potential for exploiting fresh opportunities.

   Frequently ☐ occasionally ☐ rarely ☐

3. The corporate culture is incompatible with the changing dynamics of the marketplace. And your personnel tend to be inflexible to the shifts in customers' buying behavior.

   Frequently ☐ occasionally ☐ rarely ☐

4. You fall short in aligning business plans with the corporate culture, thereby placing business plans in jeopardy.

   Frequently ☐ occasionally ☐ rarely ☐

5. At times you tend to go against the core values, beliefs, and historical traditions that represent the organization's deep-rooted culture.

   Frequently ☐ occasionally ☐ rarely ☐

PART 3

REMEDIAL ACTIONS BASED ON PARTS 1 AND 2

The above ratings for Parts 1 and 2 are qualitative assessments of your overall ability to tune-in to your corporate culture. Based on a diagnosis of your company's situation, use the following remedies to implement corrective action:

- Determine if the existing culture is compatible with the long-term vision and objectives of the organization.
- If a cultural change is required, utilize meaningful symbols, signs, and rituals to either force rapid change or make a gradual transformation.
- Determine which intrinsic qualities of your organization's culture are unique and could form a distinctive identity for use as a differentiation strategy.
- Through cross-functional teams, open communications, and a total customer orientation, utilize the diverse talents of your employees to shape a healthy corporate culture.
- Consciously align your business plan with your corporate culture.

Remedies and actions:______________________________

____

____

Executive Comments
Related to Rule 6

"An element of arrogance in our company's culture leads some managers to ignore the intense competition."

"We need to energize management and smooth over customers."

"We must meld clashing cultures and heal the rifts."

STRATEGY RULE 7: DEVELOP LEADERSHIP SKILLS

PART I

INDICATIONS THAT STRATEGY RULE 7 FUNCTIONS EFFECTIVELY

1. You understand that leadership means inspiring your people, organizing actions, developing strategies, and responding to market and competitive issues rapidly and effectively.

   Frequently ☐ occasionally ☐ rarely ☐

2. You display superior leadership skills by openly communicating to your personnel a clear vision, purpose, and direction for the business unit or company.

   Frequently ☐ occasionally ☐ rarely ☐

3. You score high in interpersonal skills, as well as in your ability to recognize the inherent dignity and worth of those you manage.

   Frequently ☐ occasionally ☐ rarely ☐

4. As a leader, you demonstrate to your staff an expertise at developing competitive strategies.

   Frequently ☐ occasionally ☐ rarely ☐

5. You reveal leadership skills in motivating your employees to win – to win customers and sustain a long-term profitable position in the marketplace.

   Frequently ☐ occasionally ☐ rarely ☐

6. You show superior leadership by helping subordinates grow and succeed through ongoing training and coaching.

   Frequently ☐ occasionally ☐ rarely ☐

7. You recognize that there is no single leadership style. Instead, a competitive environment exists that requires a personalized and flexible managerial style.

   Frequently ☐ occasionally ☐ rarely ☐

PART 2

SYMPTOMS THAT STRATEGY RULE 7 IS FUNCTIONING INEFFECTIVELY

1. Personnel tend to mistrust your ability to correctly assess market and competitive conditions and thereby make timely and accurate decisions.

   Frequently ☐ occasionally ☐ rarely ☐

2. Employees exhibit negative behavior, confusion, and an unwillingness to take the initiative.

   Frequently ☐ occasionally ☐ rarely ☐

3. The organization or business unit is enveloped by a general malaise that creates high levels of stress and anxiety.

   Frequently ☐ occasionally ☐ rarely ☐

4. You do not have an effective system of recognition and rewards.

   Frequently ☐ occasionally ☐ rarely ☐

5. Employees show excessive fears of losing: losing pride in the organization, losing status, losing in the eyes of their peers, or possibly losing employment.

   Frequently ☐ occasionally ☐ rarely ☐

6. Subordinates are rarely asked for input; and if offered, feedback is seldom given.

   Frequently ☐ occasionally ☐ rarely ☐

7. Overall, your leadership style tends to be inconsistent with the company's core values.

   Frequently ☐ occasionally ☐ rarely ☐

PART 3

REMEDIAL ACTIONS BASED ON PARTS 1 AND 2

The above ratings for Parts 1 and 2 are qualitative assessments of your overall ability to use leadership skills. Based on a diagnosis of your company's situation, use the following remedies to implement corrective action:

- Communicate to staff a vision for the firm (or business unit) so that they can picture their individual roles in the organization's long-term outlook.
- Permit individuals to act on their own initiative.
- Motivate employees to improve their skills by means of ongoing training and individual coaching.
- Create unity of effort through discipline and fostering a team effort.
- Develop a leadership style that harmonizes with the culture of the organization, objectives to be achieved, and strategies to be employed.

Executive Comments
Related to Rule 7

"Worried over complacency. Also concerned over the sharp drop in orders due to the crisis in the industry."

"With the competition circling, it's clear that complacency is a luxury we can't afford."

"Our market is still in the dumper, ensuring yet another loss. There's also a lack of cohesiveness and focus."

STRATEGY RULE 8: CREATE A MORALE ADVANTAGE

PART I

INDICATIONS THAT STRATEGY RULE 8 FUNCTIONS EFFECTIVELY

1. You actively seek to heighten morale and use it to energize the staff, tap their inner strengths, and get them to act decisively under competitive pressures.

   Frequently ☐ occasionally ☐ rarely ☐

2. You recognize that high morale holds a team together, affects day-to-day employee performance, and contributes ultimately to how well a business plan is implemented.

   Frequently ☐ occasionally ☐ rarely ☐

3. You understand that even with cutting-edge technology and outstanding business strategies, your efforts will languish if employees are not roused with the driving will to succeed.

   Frequently ☐ occasionally ☐ rarely ☐

4. You recognize that to be successful as a manager, you need to do the following to boost morale: (a) emphasize ethical standards of behavior, (b) encourage constructive communications, (c) reward individuals for meaningful performance, and (d) use a cross-functional team to encourage innovation.

   Frequently ☐ occasionally ☐ rarely ☐

5. With morale affecting day-to-day employee performance, you try to create a work environment that fosters creative thinking and encourages employees to offer opinions and ideas – with the assurance they will be given serious attention.

   Frequently ☐ occasionally ☐ rarely ☐

6. You move rapidly to overturn any skepticism shown by employees about the organization's commitment to meaningful change; and you do so before it festers into a morale problem.

   Frequently ☐ occasionally ☐ rarely ☐

PART 2

SYMPTOMS THAT STRATEGY RULE 8 IS FUNCTIONING INEFFECTIVELY

1. Employees visibly display a lack of respect toward their leadership.

   Frequently ☐ occasionally ☐ rarely ☐

2. Employees feel insecure about their jobs and have doubts about management's concern for their well-being.

   Frequently ☐ occasionally ☐ rarely ☐

3. Some key managers don't seem to be concerned about morale and their employees are generally left to fend for themselves.

   Frequently ☐ occasionally ☐ rarely ☐

4. There is no sign of a cohesive team spirit.

   Frequently ☐ occasionally ☐ rarely ☐

5. There is a conspicuous lack of new ideas, innovations, or opportunities bubbling-up to management, as well as a noticeable absence of a workable two-way communications system.

   Frequently ☐ occasionally ☐ rarely ☐

6. No consistent procedure is present to encourage and reward employees for innovative suggestions.

   Frequently ☐ occasionally ☐ rarely ☐

7. Employees exhibit erratic behavior, such as discouragement, indifference, fear, and resistance to taking risk.

   Frequently ☐ occasionally ☐ rarely ☐

8. Where new market initiatives and competitive encounters have generally failed, management routinely and primarily blames poor employee performance.

   Frequently ☐ occasionally ☐ rarely ☐

PART 3

REMEDIAL ACTIONS BASED ON PARTS 1 AND 2

The above ratings for Parts 1 and 2 are qualitative assessments of your overall ability to build morale. Based on a diagnosis of your company's situation, use the following remedies to implement corrective action:

- Communicate a long-term positive vision for the organization with clearly-stated objectives that employees can internalize and get excited about.
- Develop a learning environment that demonstrates to employees management's interest and support in their development.
- Remove any personal and physical barriers that would prevent employees from gaining pride in their work and the organization.
- Create collaborative cross-functional teams with specific duties and responsibilities.
- Encourage constructive communication up and down the organization where self-expression and innovation are encouraged.
- Nurture a corporate culture, which impacts morale, especially when it is reinforced by an ethical climate and secured by the company's positive history and core values.
- Utilize such media tools as social networking to identify where interactions take place and with whom.
- Require teams to submit strategic business plans, which serve as a unifying activity to allow collaboration and team dynamics to flourish through creative expression.

Remedies and actions:______________________________________

____

____

Executive Comments
Related to Rule 8

"With consolidation throughout the industry and a more competitive environment, there is a need to squeeze savings, cut jobs, and close branches. Yet, it's imperative that we keep employee morale up and reassure customers that they won't be abandoned."

"We've stumbled badly because of shoddy quality. Now we must get our people behind the product line, play down the tarnished name, improve quality, and set prices a bit below the market leaders."

STRATEGY RULE 9: STRENGTHEN YOUR DECISION-MAKING CAPABILITIES

PART I

INDICATIONS THAT STRATEGY RULE 9 FUNCTIONS EFFECTIVELY

1. You actively strengthen your decision-making capability by systematically examining the best practices of other companies and using them as resources to build additional layers of knowledge.

   Frequently ☐ occasionally ☐ rarely ☐

2. Where reliable competitive intelligence is lacking, you tend to rely with confidence on your innate intuition, experience, training, and knowledge to arrive at valid decisions.

   Frequently ☐ occasionally ☐ rarely ☐

3. To enhance the decision-making skills of front-line employees, you give them free reign to develop their imaginations and intuitions.

   Frequently ☐ occasionally ☐ rarely ☐

4. You understand that by valuing your organization's business history and by managing knowledge, you add greater precision to your decision-making skills.

   Frequently ☐ occasionally ☐ rarely ☐

PART 2

SYMPTOMS THAT STRATEGY RULE 9 IS FUNCTIONING INEFFECTIVELY

1. You have no organized effort to capture and record the valuable lessons and key strategies of past events and pass them on to the next generation of decision-making employees.

   Frequently ☐ occasionally ☐ rarely ☐

2. You do not have a systematic procedure or venue for individuals to share their experiences, insights, knowledge, and observations.

   Frequently ☐ occasionally ☐ rarely ☐

3. Many staff members tend to flounder and become dispirited when faced with an intense competitive situation.

   Frequently ☐ occasionally ☐ rarely ☐

PART 3

REMEDIAL ACTIONS BASED ON PARTS 1 AND 2

The above ratings for Parts 1 and 2 are qualitative assessments of your overall ability to improve the decision-making capabilities of all personnel. Based on a diagnosis of your company's situation, use the following remedies to implement corrective action:

- Provide training sessions where key individuals are invited to provide their insights and experiences.
- Set up databases that capture case histories and details of significant business events, as well as noteworthy competitive encounters – both successful and failed ones.
- Permit individuals to access the assembled information for their personal use, to coach others, and for use in formal training.

Remedies and actions:____________________________________

____

____

Executive Comments
Related to Rule 9

"The business is floundering due to a lack of cohesiveness and focus."

"Merchandise isn't moving and customers are shopping elsewhere."

"We're zigzagging between two conflicting goals: market share or profits."

"We need experience in joint ventures, mergers, and other types of alliances if we're going to succeed as a global competitor."

SUMMARY

This Strategy Diagnostic Tool is a three-dimensional view consisting of (1) the human element that elevates the natural worth of people, (2) the company's culture that determines if your plans can succeed, and (3) the implementation of strategies that decide the success of a product line, business unit, or the company.

If you merge them into a solid platform that characterizes you and your leadership, there will be ample opportunities for growth.